WILLIAM McGONAGALL

A
SELECTION

Edited by

Colin S. K. Walker

Birlinn

Foreword and brief biography copyright ©
Colin S.K. Walker, 1993, 1998

This edition first published by
Birlinn Limited 1993
Reprinted 1998 and 2003

Birlinn Limited
West Newington House
10 Newington Road
Edinburgh EH9 1QS

e-mail: info@birlinn.co.uk.
Website: http://www.birlinn.co.uk.

Typeset by Frances Gilbert
Printed and bound in Great Britain
by Cox & Wyman Ltd, Reading

A CIP record for this book is available
from The British Library

ISBN 1 874744 11 4

CONTENTS

FOREWORD

William McGonagall, self-styled poet and tragedian, has been known for many years as Scotland's 'Alternative National Bard'. He has always been a figure of fun — somebody to be mocked and certainly not to be taken seriously. Whilst much scholastic attention has been paid to Burns and others, McGonagall has rarely merited a second glance by the majority of us, save as a party piece to amuse others with. Undoubtedly, a little more would be learned concerning the realms of human compassion, as well as the mechanics of poetry, if more people were to study his work. His easily ridiculed poetry has meant that all too few people have recognized the man and his work as a rich and fruitful area of study, worthy of attention.

I have specially selected pieces from his works which not only epitomise his style but also reflect the preoccupations and concerns of the Victorian age which influenced him. I have grouped the selected verses into seven different sections, each of which taps a deep reservoir of thematically similar material. These themes draw heavily upon his own character, his cultural roots, and the contemporary history of the period. Each section has a brief introduction, setting the background to the poems and hopefully providing some insight into the diverse influences upon McGonagall's writing.

Along with this selection I have also included some extracts from autobiographical sketches which accompanied McGonagall's original works.

McGonagall's poetry is undeniably dreadful, always sinking to new depths, just when you think you have hit rock bottom. It is this inimitable multi-faceted awfulness which makes his work memorably funny. He is without question the 'Bard of the Lead Balloon'.

To examine McGonagall's work properly is to discover the criteria against which we normally judge good poetry; to explore some of the historic influences of the Victorian era, and to gain some insight into human nature and the mechanics of unconscious humour. His peculiar random calypso-like disregard for metre and use of tortuous rhymes act like signposts for the student of verse and almost define correct traditional poetical form by signally failing to meet it themselves. Much of the humour in his verse is created by the effortless manner with which McGonagall never fails to miss the mark. By concentrating on themes such as death, battle, disaster, temperance and so on we not only see vignettes of Victorian history, but also those subjects which they considered of merit to report. Perhaps the most important insight one gains by studying McGonagall's poetry is into the realms of humour and human nature. Much of the intentional humour which comes from his poetry stems from the relationship between his social background and the style in which he chose to write. Hamish Henderson provides what I think is the most accurate interpretation of McGonagall's legacy from his Scots-Irish background when he says—

> "If one listens to the productions of Irish
> 'come-all-ye' folk poets, one realises at once
> what McGonagall derived from them.
> The sinuous drawling tones which can
> accommodate umpteen words per line provide
> him with his characteristically elongated line;
> the stock subjects of battle, disaster, eulogy
> and lament provide him with his themes;
> the occasional delicious pancake drop into

6

> *deadpan flatness provided him - unconsciously*
> *I am sure - with his characteristic gimmick.*
> *It is this last feature of the 'come-ye-all' –*
> *the pantaloon fall with a thickening sud –*
> *which is present in McGonagall's work*
> *in classic form."* [1]

Unfortunately, whilst the roots of McGonagall's verse are firmly embedded in the tradition of Irish 'come-all-ye' folk poetry, he has tried to graft onto them the language and vocabulary of more refined Victorian art poetry. It is the resulting hybrid which provides us with the humour. Listening to his poetry is like observing somebody digging up the road wearing formal evening dress. It is the incongruity which immediately brings a smile to one's face. However, reading the autobiographical sketches wipes the smile off again when we notice that McGonagall is completely oblivious to his *faux pas*, for the whole tone of these autobiographical fragments is touchingly solemn without a hint of humour or self-satire. In his naïveté, he even went as far as to proudly print alongside his own verses a transparently cynical 'Tribute from Three Students at Glasgow University' in which, among other questions they asked him:

> *"Is the most intellectual benefit to be derived*
> *from a study of the McGonagallian or*
> *Shakespearian school of poetry?"*

It has been suggested that he was not as naïve as it would appear, and merely played the part of fool whilst making a living from its proceeds. I disagree; McGonagall was not one to play the fool –he took his work and his creations seriously and had an invincible belief in his own genius.

7

He once said:

*"I have nailed the colours of my political
genius to the mast of my own appreciation,
and twenty thousand demons in the shape
of adverse critics cannot rend them assunder."*

I fear rather, that his single-minded belief in his own poetical prowess coupled with a touching innocence created a world for him in which he was oblivious to the mockery until it was too late. Instead of mocking him one should perhaps give him a little praise for the boundless generosity of his character, for he was always willing to think well of people until proven wrong. Victorian art poetry and Irish folk poetry have their respected places in our cultural heritage as does the art of Thespian performance, but somehow McGonagall's mixture of these components produced a queer mongrel which, true to his sense of bathos, is less than the sum of its constituent parts.

Reading the autobiographical sketches, one becomes acutely aware of how cruel his Victorian audience was and feel somewhat ashamed for laughing at his unintentional humour. In the end, what provides the secret of McGonagall's durability is the fact that no one has written, or could write as badly 'if they tried'. This said, I would also defy anyone to perform them as well as the creator himself.

In some respects his work defies complete analysis, for the very qualities we seek to understand and explain were not intended by the artist himself, nor do they appear to come wholly from his subconscious - they are epiphenomena. In reading what follows I trust that as well as enjoying a good laugh at the sheer awfulness of it all, you

8

also gain some appreciation that McGonagall was an interesting character writing in an interesting era and is worthy of more attention than he has perhaps hitherto received.

Colin S.K.Walker

[1]Hamish Henderson "McGonagall the What" p.276 in "Alias MacAlias" Edinburgh: Polygon, 1992

BRIEF BIOGRAPHY

William McGonagall was born in Edinburgh in 1825 (he actually left two dates of birth in his autobiographical accounts; research shows 1825 to be likelier than 1830), the son of an immigrant Irish cotton weaver. It would appear that due to the economic climate, his father was forced to move in search of employment several times during McGonagall's early years. However, much of his childhood was spent on the Orkney island of South Ronaldsay until, aged eleven, the family moved to Dundee where he eventually joined his father as a handloom weaver. On the 11th July 1846 he married Jean King. Having spent much of his youth reading Shakespeare's 'penny' plays, McGonagall was always interested in the theatre, and became a keen amateur actor, often performing to an audience of work colleagues. He joined in productions with the travelling troupes who visited Dundee's Theatre Royal, playing the characters of Macbeth, Hamlet, Othello, and Richard III. It is reported that in 1872, he gave three performances a night as Macbeth until he was hoarse voiced, and that once, when performing at the Theatre Royal, he became so carried away with the part that he refused to die when Macduff stabbed him.

1877 was the year in which the most startling and influential event took place in McGonagall's life– when he was already 52 years old. It took place in his back room in Paton's Lane in Dundee on a holiday in June, when he was lamenting not being able to get away to the Highlands. Suddenly he was seized by the 'not-to-be-denied' calling to be a poet. He writes:

"... all of a sudden my body got inflamed, and
instantly I was seized with a strong desire to

11

write poetry, so strong, in fact, that in imag-
ination I thought I heard a voice crying in my
ears– 'Write! Write!'"

From that day, he resolved to give up his loom to peddle
the poems which poured forth from his 'inflamed' body.
1878 saw the publication of his first collection of poems
which included the popular 'Railway Bridge of the Sil-
very Tay'.

McGonagall believed that it was his duty to perform
his works, and from then on, he travelled central Scotland
giving public recitations and selling his poetry in broad-
sheets. He continued to pursue the life of poet and
performer, even although the rewards were meagre and
his wife begged him return to handloom weaving. As a
result, his poor illiterate wife was forced to find work in
the laundry of the Dundee Asylum.

In Edinburgh McGonagall became very popular with
the student fraternity who, unbeknownst to him, delighted
in setting him up as the butt of their pranks and jokes.
Likewise, he was made fun of in his adopted home of
Dundee, where several of the local dignitaries were so
embarassed to have his name associated with the city that
they suggested that he leave. He visited London in 1880,
and even emigrated to New York in 1887. However, this,
as with many other things in his life, proved unsuccessful,
and, stopping only for a brief time in Glasgow whilst in
transit from America, he eventually returned to Dundee.
McGonagall continued to live and perform here for about
six or seven years, making public appearances at Baron
Ziegler's Circus. His most famous collection of verses
'Poetic Gems' was first published in 1890. Unfortunately
his ever perilous financial affairs forced him to look
elsewhere to ply his trade, so he moved to Perth in search

of a more appreciative audience. Sadly he found few people here who were willing to buy his broadsheets, and ended up poorer than ever. In these dire circumstances, he was contemplating a return to Dundee when some admirers from his native city persuaded him to return to Edinburgh. Here he was to stay for the remainder of his life. In his last years he liked to be known as 'Sir William Topaz McGonagall; Knight of the White Elephant' which was a spurious title conferred upon him by some mischevious students from Edinburgh purporting to be from King Theebaw of Burmah and the Andaman Islands. He died in Edinburgh, the city of his birth, on the 29th September 1902 and was buried in Greyfriars Kirkyard.

SELECTED EXTRACTS FROM
AUTOBIOGRAPHICAL SKETCHES

SIR WILLIAM TOPAZ McGONAGALL
POET AND TRAGEDIAN

Knight of the White Elephant, Burmah

My Dear Readers of this autobiography, which I am the author of, I beg leave to inform you that I was born in Edinburgh. My parents were born in Ireland, and my father was a handloom weaver, and he learned me the handloom weaving while in Dundee, and I followed it for many years, until it began to fail owing to machinery doing the weaving instead of the handloom. So much so as I couldn't make a living from it. But I may say Dame Fortune has been very kind to me by endowing me with the genius of poetry. I remember how I felt when I received the spirit of poetry. It was in the year of 1877, and in the month of June, when trees and flowers were in full bloom. Well, it being the holiday week in Dundee, I was sitting in my back room in Paton's Lane, Dundee, lamenting to myself because I couldn't get to the Highlands on holiday to see the beautiful scenery, when all of a sudden my body got inflamed, and instantly I was seized with a strong desire to write poetry, so strong, in fact, that in imagination I thought I heard a voice crying in my ears—
"WRITE! WRITE!"
I wondered what could be the matter with me, and I began to walk backwards and forwards in a great fit of excitement, saying to myself— "I know nothing about poetry." But still the voice kept ringing in my ears —"Write, write," until at last, being overcome with a desire to write poetry,

I found paper, pen, and ink, and in a state of frenzy, sat me down to think what would be my first subject for a poem. All at once I thought of the late Rev. George Gilfillan, and composed a poem of four stanzas in his praise as a preacher, and orator, and poet. Then I sent it to the "Weekly News" for publication, not sending my name with it, only my initials – W. M'G., Dundee. It was published, along with a short comment by the editor in its praise, as follows:– *"W. M'G., Dundee, has sent us a poem in praise of the Rev. George Gilfillan, and he sung his praises truly and well, but he modestly seeks to hide his light under a bushel,"* so when I read the poem in the "Weekly News" I was highly pleased no doubt to see such a favourable comment regarding it. Then my next poem, or second, was the "Railway Bridge of the Silvery Tay," which caused a great sensation in Dundee and far away. In fact, gentle readers, it was the only poem that made me famous universally. The reading of the poem abroad caused the Emperor of Brazil to leave his home far away incognito and view the bridge as he passed along *en route* to Inverness. But, my dear readers, the Tay Bridge poem is out of print, and I do not intend to publish it again, owing to the fall of the bridge in the year of 1879, which will be remembered for a very long time.

I may also state in this short autobiography of mine that my parents are dead some years ago– I don't remember how many, but they are buried in the Eastern Necropolis, Dundee, and I may say they were always good to me.

And now concerning something more attractive, my dear readers, I must inform ye that as early as ten years of age I was very fond of reading Shakespeare's Penny Plays (Vicker's edition), and from them I received great knowledge regarding the histrionic art. The plays or tragedies I studied most were Macbeth, Hamlet, Richard III, and Othello, the Moor of Venice, and these four characters I have impersonated in my time. During my stay in Dundee my

FIRST APPEARANCE ON THE STAGE

was in the character of Macbeth in Mr Giles' Penny Theatre, Lindsay Street, Dundee, to an overflowing and crowded audience, and I received unbounded applause. I was called before the curtain several times during the performance, and I remember the actors of the company felt very jealous owing to me getting the general applause, and several were as bold as tell me so; and when it came to the combat scene betwixt me and Macduff the actor who was playing Macduff against my Macbeth tried to spoil me in the combat by telling me to cut it short, so as the audience, in his opinion, would say it was a poor combat, but I was too cute for him, guessing his motive for it. I continued the combat until he was fairly exhausted, and until there was one old gentleman in the audience cried out, "Well done, M'Gonagall! Walk into him!" And so I did until he was in a great rage, and stamped his foot, and cried out, "Fool! Why don't you fall?" And when I did fall the cry was "M'Gonagall! M'Gonagall! Bring him out! Bring him out!" until I had to come before the curtain and receive an ovation from the audience. Such was the case in my second appearance, under the management of Forrest Knowles in the Grocers' Hall, Castle Street, Dundee. The characters I appeared in under his management were Macbeth, Richard III, and Hamlet. These three characters I performed to crowded and delighted audiences. I remember Mr Knowles told me in the dressing-room that I looked the character so well in the dress that

17

I should wear it, and not throw it off, but I told him it was too great a joke to say so. I also remember on that night there were several gentlemen in the audience who were from Edinburgh, and they came to my dressing-room to congratulate me on my great success, and shook hands with me, telling me that few professionals could do it so well; but perhaps they were only flattering me. If so, I will say with the poet, John Dryden –

Flattery, like ice, our footing does betray,
Who can tread sure on the smooth slippery way ?
Pleased with the fancy, we glide swiftly on,
And see the dangers which we cannot shun.

Well, my dear friends, the next event in my life that I am going to relate is regarding me and my Mistress M'Gonagall leaving Dundee in the year 1894, resolving to return no more owing to the harsh treatment I had received in the city, as is well known for a truth without me recording it. Well, I went to the Fair City of Perth, one of the finest upon the earth, intending to remain there altogether. So I secured a small garret in the South Street, and me and my mistress lived there for eight months, and the inhabitants were very kind to us in many respects...

My Dear Readers,– I must now tell ye my reason for leaving the Fair City of Perth. It was because I found it to be too small for me making a living in. I must allow, the inhabitants were very kind to me during my stay amongst them. And while living there I received a letter, and when I opened it I was struck with amazement when I found a silver elephant enclosed, and I looked at it in amazement, and said– "I'll now have a look at this big letter enclosed." I was astonished to see that King Theebaw, of Burmah and the Andaman Islands, had conferred upon me the honorary title of Sir Wm. Topaz M'Gonagall, Knight of The White Elephant, Burmah, and for the benefit of my readers and the public, I consider I am justified in recording it in my autobiography, which runs as follows:–

Dear and Most Highly Honoured Sir,– Having the great honour to belong to the same holy fraternity of poets as yourself, I have been requested by our fellow-countrymen at present serving our Queen and country in Her Majesty's great Indian Empire to send you the following address, and at the same time to inform you that you were lately appointed a Grand Knight of the Holy Order of the White Elephant, Burmah, by his Royal Highness upon representation being made to him by your fellow-countrymen out here.

King Theebaw, who is just now holding his Court in the Andaman Islands, expressed himself as being only too pleased to confer the highest honour possible upon merit, wheresoever found, if that merit were judged worthy by his Grand Topaz General. As the latter gentleman has long been impressed by the injustice with which you have been treated by your great modesty upon several occasions has been noticed by His Royal Highness the King of Burmah, it gives him great pleasure to assure Theebaw, the King, that none more worthy of this high honour has ever lived in the East, whereat His Royal Highness called his Court together, and with much eclat and esteem caused it to be proclaimed throughout his present palace and kingdom that you were to be known henceforth as Topaz M'Gonagall, G.K.H.O.W.E.B.

Should you ever visit the Andaman Islands it will be his great pleasure to be presented to you, and to do all honour to you, according to very ancient custom with which members of our mutual illustrious Order have always been treated by his ancestors.

That you will consent to accept the high honour now offered to you is the wish nearest the hearts of your countrymen in the East; that you may be long spared to enrich British literature by your grand and thrilling works is their most sincere prayer.

His Majesty also expressed it as his opinion, and the opinion of his grandfathers as far back as the flood, that such talented works as those of their holy fraternity of poets were, had always been, and for ever would be, above all earthly praise, their value being inestimable. He further stated that he failed to conceive how Rosebery could have been so blind as not to have offered to such a man as yourself the paltry and mean stipend attached to the position of Poet Laureate of Great Britain and Ireland. It is indescribable to him that any man of ordinary rummel gumption could possibly offer remuneration to such a gift of the Gods as yours.

Should you see fit to do the ancient Kingdom of Burmah the honour of accepting the Ribbon of its highest Order, and will kindly pay its capital a visit at your earliest convenience, it is the King's order that you be received with all the ceremony due to the greatest ornament now living of the Holy Order of the White Elephant. You are to be immediately installed in the holy chair of the Knights of the above Order upon arrival, from which it is the custom of the holy fraternity to address the whole Eastern world.

King Theebaw will not injure your sensitive feelings by offering you any filthy lucre as payment for what you may compose in his honour after receiving the insignia of the Holy Order. He also states it will be his duty to see that your name is duly reverenced throughout the Kingdom.

I have the honour to be, most noble and illustrious sir, your most humble brother in the fraternity of poets.

(Per) C.MACDONALD, K.O.W.E.B.,
Poet Laureate of Burmah.

By order of His Royal Highness the King.

Topaz General.
Topaz Minister.
Secretary of State.
Holder of Seals.
Registrar-General.
Staff-Bearer.
Secretary of Letters Patent.
Keeper of the White Elephant.

My dear readers, this letter regarding my knighthood is a correct copy from the original as near as I can write it, with the exception of the Indian language therein, which means the names of the gentlemen that signed the Royal patent letter regarding my knighthood. That is all that is wanting, which I cannot write or imitate. Nor can I imitate the four red seals that are affixed to the Royal document. The insignia of the knighthood is a silver elephant attached to a green silk ribbon.

This, my dear readers, is the full particulars regarding my Indian knighthood, and, my dear friends and well-wishers, I must conclude this autobiography of mine by truthfully recording herein that since I came to beautiful Edinburgh, and that is more than six years now past, I have received the very best of treatment, and during my stay in Edinburgh I have given many entertainments from my own poetic works, also from Shakespeare.

I may say I have been highly appreciated by select audiences, and for their appreciation of my abilities I return them my sincere thanks for being so kind as to give me their support since I came to Edinburgh.– My dear friends, I am, yours faithfully,

SIR Wm. TOPAZ M'GONAGALL,
Poet and Knight of the White Elephant,
Burmah.

PART I

All hail to the Empress of India
Great Britain's Queen

McGonagall's poetry can clearly be seen to be 'Victorian' by his choice of subject matter. Nowhere is this more obvious than in this first section, where I have especially chosen poems which he wrote about Queen Victoria herself. Born on May 24th 1819 at Kensington Palace, she reigned longer than any other British monarch. On her accession to the throne in 1837, McGonagall was already twelve years old; he was to experience forty years of her reign before the muse struck him and he decided to be a poet. Whilst she was on the throne, 1837-1901, Great Britain was to become the most powerful industrial nation in the world, and the centre of the greatest Empire known. What better time could there have been to inspire a poet with as fully a developed sense of royalism and patriotism as McGonagall had?

In 1877, the year in which he heard the "not-to-be-denied" call to "Write ! Write !", McGonagall undertook to secure the Royal patronage of Queen Victoria with his verse **"A Requisition to the Queen"**. Along with the "Requisition" he sent, as an example of his poetical prowess, "An Address to Shakespeare". Shakespeare was the only poet who McGonagall held in high regard. He had once, when being complimented by certain of his admirers who assured him he had not his equal in the world, modestly admitted the truth of this, but claimed one exception. He said:

> *"I bow the knee to Shakespeare,*
> *but to no other poet, living or dead !"*

In return for these unsolicited offerings, McGonagall received a letter from Sir Thomas Biddulph, Captain of the Queen's Household, thanking him on the Queen's behalf, but saying that she was not able to keep such gifts and hence he was returning them. McGonagall interpreted this as "Her Majesty's Royal Letter of patronage for my poetic abilities", and proudly printed "Patronised by Her Majesty" at the top of all his broadsheets.

In 1878, McGonagall undertook an arduous journey on foot to visit the Queen whilst she was staying in Scotland at Balmoral. Like so many of his enterprises, this pilgrimage, for that is what it amounted to, was doomed to failure. After two nights on the road, enduring many hardships along the way, he got no further than the guard on the gate at Balmoral, who turned him away. The poet returned the way he had come, and arrived back in Dundee three days later, "footsore and weary, but not in the least discouraged".

The **"Royal Review"** sees two of McGonagall's favourite subjects– Queen Victoria and the Military– come together at an event which, despite his efforts at raising it to the status of a grand event, was clearly a washout. On the 25th August 1881 the Scottish Volunteer Force "celebrated" its twenty first anniversary with a Royal Review at Holyrood park in Edinburgh. Unfortunately this was a notable year for terrible storms the length and breadth of the country, and this event certainly did not escape the wrath of the bad weather, for the rain fell in torrents throughout the day, turning the parade ground into a quagmire. The disappointing nature of the event, coupled with McGonagall's usual disregard for conventional poetic form, come together marvellously in this poem to create something truly awful. The all pervading sense of anticlimax is so great that one almost needs a bathysphere to plumb the depths of its bathos.

On March 2nd 1882, Queen Victoria was nearly assassinated on the platform of Windsor station by a madman named Roderick Maclean, who fired off a pistol in her direction, but missed. Maclean was tried for the crime a few weeks later, found not guilty on the ground of insanity and sent to Broadmoor. However, Queen Victoria was incensed at the verdict and reportedly said "Insane he may have been, but not guilty he most certainly was not, as I saw him fire the pistol myself ". The Prime Minister Mr. Gladstone succumbed to the Queen's wishes and without even trying to explain the correctness of the law, passed an act in 1883 which changed the wording of the verdict to one commonly known as "Guilty but Insane". The attempted assassination was an occasion which illicited great popular sympathy and McGonagall, whose generous hearted allegiance had in no way been shaken by his Balmoral experience, rose heartily to the event with his poem **"Attempted Assassination of the Queen"**.

McGonagall's poetry covers both of the Queen's Jubilees– her Golden one in 1887, and the Diamond one ten years later marking 60 years of her reign. In this selection I include his ode to **"The Queen's Diamond Jubilee Celebrations"**. These celebrations were more far reaching than the earlier Golden ones, as this time they encompassed colonial dignitaries from all around the globe, as well as the crowned heads of Europe, most of whom were relations of Queen Victoria. The Diamond Jubilee celebrations saw the beginning of a new era– the "British Commonwealth of Nations". Although McGonagall describes the events, people, and places with his customary attention to detail, he did not attend the celebrations himself. This might at first appear strange for a travelling bard who had always showed unswerving loyalty to, and admiration for, his sovereign. However, in 1897 Queen Victoria had only four more years to live, McGonagall five. He had returned to his native Edinburgh by this time, and as well as being penniless (not something which would have normally deterred him from travelling) his correspondence reveals that he also faced the hurdle of being dogged by ill health in the latter stages of his life. Hence, it is perhaps not so surprising that he did not manage to undertake a personal pilgrimage to London. This section ends suitably with **"The Death of the Queen"**, which occurred on January 22nd 1901, barely more than eighteen months before McGonagall was himself to die. It must be mentioned that although his health was poor he still continued to write. The last verses he wrote were in celebration of the Coronation of the new King Edward VII, written a fortnight before McGonagall died on 29th September 1902.

A REQUISITION TO THE QUEEN

Smiths Buildings No. 19
Patons Lane,
Sept the 6th. 1877.

1. Most August! Empress of India,
        and of great Britain the Queen,
I most humbly beg your pardon, hoping you
        will not think it mean
That a poor poet that lives in Dundee,
Would be so presumptous to write unto Thee.

2. Most lovely Empress of India,
        and Englands generous Queen,
I send you an Address, I have written on
        Scotlands Bard,
Hoping that you will accept it,
        and not be with me to hard,
Nor fly into a rage,but be as Kind
        and Condescending
As to give me your Patronage

3. Beautiful Empress, of India,
        and Englands Gracious Queen,
I send you a Shakespearian Address
        written by me.
And I think if your Majesty reads it,
        right pleased you will be.
And my heart it will leap with joy, if it is
        patronized by Thee.

4. Most Mighty Empress, of India,
      and Englands beloved Queen,
Most Handsome to be Seen.
I wish you every Success.
And that heaven may you bless.

For your Kindness to the poor while
      they are in distress.
I hope the Lord will protect you while living
And hereafter when your Majesty is ... dead.
I hope Thee Lord above will place an eternal
      Crown upon your Head.
I am your Gracious Majesty ever faithfull to Thee,
William McGonagall, The Poor Poet,
      That lives in Dundee.

THE ROYAL REVIEW
AUGUST 25, 1881

All hail to the Empress of India,
  Great Britain's Queen–
Long may she live in health, happy and serene–
  That came from London, far away,
To review the Scottish Volunteers in grand array:
  Most magnificent to be seen,
Near by Salisbury Crags and its pastures green,
Which will long be remembered by our gracious
  Queen–

And by the Volunteers, that came from far away,
Because it rain'd most of the day.
And with the rain their clothes were wet all
  through,
On the 25th day of August, at the Royal Review.
And to the Volunteers it was no lark,
Because they were ankle deep in mud in the
  Queen's Park,
Which proved to the Queen they were loyal and
  true,
To ensure such hardship at the Royal Review.

Oh! it was a most beautiful scene
To see the Forfarshire Artillery marching past
  the Queen;
Her Majesty with their steady marching felt
  content,
Especially when their arms to her they did present.

And the Inverness Highland Volunteers seemed
   very gran',
And marched by steady to a man
Amongst the mud without dismay,
And the rain pouring down on them all the way.
And the bands they did play, God Save the Queen,
Near by Holyrood Palace and the Queen's Park so
   green.

Success to our noble Scottish Volunteers!
I hope they will be spared for many long years,
And to Her Majesty always prove loyal and true,
As they have done for the second time at the
   Royal Review.

To take them in general, they behaved very well,
The more that the rain fell on them pell-mell.
They marched by Her Majesty in very grand array,
Which will be remembered for many a long day,
Bidding defiance to wind and rain,
Which adds the more fame to their name.

And I hope none of them will have cause to rue
The day that they went to the Royal Review.
And I'm sure Her Majesty ought to feel proud,
And in her praise she cannot speak too loud,
Because the more that it did rain they did not
   mourn,
Which caused Her Majesty's heart with joy to burn,

Because she knew they were loyal and true
For enduring such hardships at the Royal Review.

ATTEMPTED ASSASSINATION OF
THE QUEEN

GOD prosper long our noble Queen,
And long may she reign!
Maclean he tried to shoot her,
But it was all in vain.

For God He turned the ball aside
Maclean aimed at her head;
And he felt very angry
Because he didn't shoot her dead.

There's divinity that hedgeth a king,
And so it does seem.
And my opinion is, it has hedged
Our most gracious Queen.

Maclean must be a madman,
Which is obvious to be seen,
Or else he wouldn't have tried to shoot
Our most beloved Queen.

Victoria is a good Queen,
Which all her subjects know,
And for that God has protected her
From all her deadly foes.

She is noble and generous,
Her subjects must confess;

There hasn't been her equal
Since the days of good Queen Bess

Long may she be spared to roam
Among the bonnie Highland floral,
And spend many a happy day
In the palace of Balmoral.

Because she is very kind
To the old women there,
And allows them bread, tea, and sugar,
And each one to get a share.

And when they know of her coming,
Their hearts feel overjoy'd,
Because, in general, she finds work
For men that's unemploy'd.

And she also gives the gipsies money
While at Balmoral, I've been told,
And, mind ye, seldom silver,
But very often gold.

I hope God will protect her
By night and by day,
At home and abroad
When she's far away.

May He be as a hedge around her,
As He's been all along,
And let her live and die in peace
Is the end of my song.

THE QUEEN'S DIAMOND JUBILEE
CELEBRATIONS

'Twas in the year of 1897, and on the 22nd of June,
Her Majesty's Diamond Jubilee in London caused
   a great boom;
Because high and low came from afar to see,
The grand celebrations at Her Majesty's
   Diamond Jubilee.

People were there from almost every foreign land,
Which made the scene really imposing and grand;
Especially the Queen's carriage, drawn by eight
   cream-coloured bays,
And when the spectators saw it joyous shouts
   they did raise.

Oh! it was a most gorgeous sight to be seen,
Numerous foreign magnates were there for to see
   the Queen;
And to the vast mutitude there of women and men,
Her Majesty for two hours showed herself to them.

The head of the procession looked very grand—
A party of the Horse Guards with their
   gold-belaced band;
Which also headed the procession of the Colonial States,
While slowly they rode on until opposite the
   Palace gates.

Then the sound of the National Anthem was heard
   quite clear,
And the sound the hearts of the mighty crowd did cheer;

As they heard the loyal hymning on the morning air,
The scene was most beautiful and surpassing fair.

On the house tops thousands of people were to be seen,
All in eager expectation of seeing the Queen;
And all of them seemed to be happy and gay,
Which enhanced the scene during the day.

And when Field Marshal Roberts in the
   procession passed by,
The cheers from thousands of people arose very high;
And to see him on his war horse was inspiring to see,
Because he rode his charger most splendidly.

The Natal mounted troops were loudly cheered,
   they looked so grand,
And also the London Irish Emerald Isle Band,
Oh it was a most magnificent sight to see.
The Malta Militia and Artillery,
And the Trinidad Artillery, and also bodies of
   infantry,
And, as the crowd gazed thereon, it filled their
   hearts with glee.

Her Majesty looked well considering her years,
And from the vast crowd burst forth joyous cheers;
And Her Majesty bowed to the shouts of acclamation,
And smiled upon the crowd with a loving look of
   admiration.

His Excellency Chan Yin Hun in his carriage was
   a great attraction,
And his Oriental garb seemed to give the people

great satisfaction;
While the two little Battenberg's carriage,
  as it drove along,
Received from the people cheering loud and long.

And when the Dragoon Guards and the Hussars
  filed past at the walk,
Then loudly in their praise the people did talk;
And the cavalry took forty minutes to trot past,
While the spectators in silent wonder stood aghast.

Her Majesty the Empress Frederick a great
  sensation made,
She was one of the chief attractions in the whole
  cavalcade;
And in her carriage was the Princess Louise,
  the Marchioness of Lorne,
In a beautiful white dress, which did her person adorn.

The scene in Piccadilly caused a great sensation,
The grand decorations there were the theme of
  admiration;
And the people in St. James Street were taken
  by surprise,
Because the lovely decorations dazzled their eyes.

The 42nd Highlanders looked very fine,
When they appeared and took up a position
  on the line;
And the magnificent decorations in the Strand,
As far east as the Griffin was attractive and grand.

And the grandstand from Buckingham Palace to
   Temple Bar,
Was crowded with eager eyes from afar,
Looking on the floral decorations and flags unfurled,
Which has been the grandest spectacle ever seen
   in the world.

The corner building of St. James Street side was
   lovely to view,
Ornamented with pink and white bunting and a
   screen of blue;
And to the eye, the inscription thereon most
   beautiful seems:
"Thou art alone the Queen of earthly Queens."

The welcome given to Commander-in-Chief
   Lord Wolseley was very flattering,
The people cheered him until the streets did ring;
And the foreign princes were watched with
   rivetted admiration,
And caused among the sight-seers great consternation.

And private householders seemed to vie with
   each other,
In the lavishness of their decorations,
   and considered it to bother;
And never before in the memory of man,
Has there been a national celebration so grand.

And in conclusion, I most earnestly do pray,
May God protect Her Majesty for many a day;
My blessing on her noble form and on her lofty head,
And may she wear a crown of glory hereafter when dead.

THE DEATH OF THE QUEEN

Alas! our noble and generous Queen Victoria is dead,
And I hope her soul to Heaven has fled,
To sing and rejoice with saints above,
Where all is joy, peace, and love.

'Twas on January 22, 1901, in the evening
   she died at 6.30 o'clock,
Which to the civilised world has been a great shock;
She was surrounded by her children and
   grandchildren dear,
And for the motherly, pious Queen they shed
   many a tear.

She has been a model and faithful Queen,
Very few like her have been;
She has acted virtuously during her long reign,
And I'm afraid the world will never see her like again.

And during her reign she was beloved by the high
   and the low,
And through her decease the people's hearts are
   full of woe,
Because she was kind to her subjects at home
   and abroad,
And now she's receiving her reward from the
   Eternal God.

And during her reign in this world of trouble and
   strife
Several attempts were made to take her life;
Maclean he tried to shoot her, but he did fail,

But he was arrested and sent to an asylum,
  which made him bewail.

Victoria was a noble Queen, the people must confess,
She was most charitable to them while in distress;
And in her disposition she wasn't proud nor vain,
And tears for her loss will fall as plentiful as rain.

The people around Balmoral will shed many tears
Owing to her visits amongst them for many years;
She was very kind to the old, infirm women there,
By giving them provisions and occasionally a
  prayer.

And while at Balmoral she found work for men
  unemployed,
Which made the hearts of the poor men
  feel overjoyed;
And for Her Majesty they would have laid down
  their lives,
Because sometimes she saved them from
  starving, and their wives.

Many happy days she spent at Balmoral,
Viewing the blooming heather and the bonnie
  Highland floral,
Along with Prince Albert, her husband dear,
But alas! when he died she shed many a tear.

She was very charitable, as everybody knows,
But the loss of her husband caused her many woes,
Because he cheered her at Balmoral as they the
  heather trod,

But I hope she has met him now at the Throne of God.
They ascended the Hill of Morven when she
  was in her fortieth year,
And Her Majesty was delighted as she
  viewed the Highland deer;
Also dark Lochnagar, which is most beautiful to see,
Not far from Balmoral and the dark River Dee.

I hope they are walking in Heaven together
  as they did in life
In the beautiful celestial regions, free from all strife,
Where God's family together continually meet,
Where the streets are paved with gold,
  and everything complete.

Alas! for the loss of Queen Victoria the
  people will mourn,
But she unto them can never return;
Therefore to mourn for her is all in vain,
Knowing that she can never return again.

Therefore, good people, one and all,
Let us be prepared for death when God
  does on us call,
Like the good and noble Queen Victoria of renown,
The greatest and most virtuous Queen that
  ever wore a crown.

PART II

Beautiful Silvery Tay

McGonagall expressed a love of Homeric epithets in his poetry, and for him, just as Dundee was always "Bonnie", the River Tay was always "Silvery". The use of such epithets was common practice among folk ballad writers in his day, who did not spend long composing their works and tended to use a stock of such well used words or phrases to fill up the lines. The repetitive use of such words meant that their simple ballads were easily remembered, by composer and audience alike. McGonagall undoubtably used this technique in his own compositions, however most of his works were not written as songs, and so we get his own peculiar style of poetry.

One might wonder why one struck with the poetic muse would settle in Dundee? It has been cynically suggested that had Dundee been built on the banks of the River Orinoco, then perhaps McGonagall would not have been quite such a prolific poet, for as well as undoubtedly inspiring his poetic soul, the Tay also provided an easy name to rhyme with. I cannot hold with such cynicism, for a poet with the determination of McGonagall would have found no difficulty in observing:

> *"...the silvery tides moving to and fro,*
> *on the banks of the majestic Orinoco !"*

No, to McGonagall the Silvery Tay was a sight which truly moved and inspired the poet within him. During his many years residence in Dundee, first in Paton's Lane and later in Step Row, McGonagall was just a stones throw from the river, and his view of the Tay would have included the building site of both of the Tay Bridges, which took place virtually at the bottom of his road. What more inspiration did he need for subject matter?

We start this section with **"The Railway Bridge of the Silvery Tay"**, which describes the first bridge over the River Tay designed by Thomas Bouch. In his autobiographical notes, McGonagall states that after the publication of this poem he was pronounced by the press "The Poet Laureate of the Tay Bridge". Was this an omen! The building of this bridge was not without its setbacks, and several accidents caused loss of life during its construction. The Tay Bridge took slightly longer than three years to build and cost over £350,000. When completed in 1877, the bridge was seen as one of the engineering achievements of the age, and when it was officially opened on May 31st 1878 the Dundee city fathers saw fit to award the Freedom of the City to the chief architect Thomas Bouch. During construction it was visited by such notables as the Emperor of Brazil and the ex-President of the United States, Ulysses S. Grant. Queen Victoria travelled over the bridge in August 1879 on her way south from Balmoral. She recorded the event in her journal thus:

"We reached the Tay Bridge Station at six.
Immense crowds everywhere, flags waving
in every direction, and the whole population
out ... The Provost splendidly attired presented
an address. We stopped here about five
minutes, and then began going over the
marvellous Tay Bridge, which is more than a
mile and a half long. Mr. Bouch who was
presented at Dundee,was the engineer. It took
us I should say about eight minutes going over.
The view was very fine."

Later she was to knight Thomas Bouch for his achievement. Knowing now what dreadful fate was to befall the structure, one is almost alarmed at the prophetic nature of McGonagall's poem in which he prays that there will never be a disaster.

Alas, his next poem "The Tay Bridge Disaster" shows us that his prayer was not answered. The disaster occurred on Sunday 28th December 1879 just after 7p.m. The weather had been getting worse all day, and by the evening there were gale force winds. As the ill fated train, Engine 224, reached the bridge the storm was at its worst and the structure was being battered by the gale. Moments later, the bridge gave way and the train and its passengers fell into the Tay. In "The Tay Bridge Disaster", McGonagall was able to write at the full stretch of his narrative powers, with horror and pathos, as well as majesty.

The sequence of bridge poems ends with "An Address to the New Tay Bridge", a fine passacaglia in which he praises the strength and beauty of the structure. These "Bridge" poems call forth most of the qualities and emotional attitudes which distinguish McGonagall's style. In these works he delights in the grandiose, the exclamatory superlatives, the effective repetitions, the topographical and chronological exactitudes, the pathos, the bathos and local patriotism. McGonagall's poetic style is fed by events, places, and sights which are on a truly gigantic scale.

In "A Descriptive Poem on the Silvery Tay", McGonagall waxes lyrical about the beautiful scenery which surrounds the river. The Tay, with the Fife country-side beyond was clearly seen as an idyllic place to escape to when one was standing with the smoking chimneys of Juteopolis at one's back. In this poem, as with the "Address to the New Tay Bridge", McGonagall makes mention of the "Mars Boys". The Industrial Schools Act of 1866 had led to the establishment of a number of training ships around the shores of the United Kingdom, and one of these was the Tay training ship "Mars". The "Mars" had enjoyed a fairly short and uneventful spell of active service before being anchored off Newport to serve as a training ship for the East of Scotland. It provided a naval type training for up to 400 young boys between the ages of 12 and 14.

In the final poem in this section **"The Famous Tay Whale"**, McGonagall gives us a contemporary account of one of Dundee's greatest legends. When the Tay whale swam up the Tay in the first week of December 1883, it was most unfortunate in its choice of rivers, for at that time, Dundee was Britain's main whaling port. The "hunchback whale", as it was known, was first harpooned on Friday 7th December 1883, and "showed face" frequently in the river, apparently giving a great exhibition of its aquatic abilities on Sunday 31st when all the whalers were at church. It was however hunted and fatally wounded on New Year's Day 1884. Not one to give in easily, the whale broke free of the harpoon lines and escaped after a twenty-two hour chase. The Tay Whale disappeared north of the Bell Rock Lighthouse and was not seen again until the 8th January when it was spotted floating upside down by some fishermen from nearby Gourdon. It was towed to Stonehaven and auctioned on the beach, where it was bought by Mr. John Woods, a Dundee oil merchant for £226. On the 11th January, the tug boat "Excelsior" towed the animal back to Dundee where it was exhibited for a while behind Mr. Wood's wooden house on wheels at the east end of Dock Street. After partial preservation, it was sent on a tour of many of the larger cities including London, Liverpool, and Glasgow. On its return to Dundee, it was dissected by Professor Struthers of Aberdeen University and its skeleton given to the local museum. McGonagall composed this poem on January 15th 1884, and would appear to have been one of the locals who paid to see the whale in John Wood's yard in Dundee. According to another contemporary reporter, the smell of the whale, let alone the sight of its huge carcase was enough to leave an indelible impression upon any witness.

THE RAILWAY BRIDGE OF THE
SILVERY TAY

BEAUTIFUL Railway bridge of the Silvery Tay!
With your numerous arches and pillars in so grand
  array,
And your central girders, which seem to the eye
To be almost towering to the sky.
The greatest wonder of the day,
And a great beautification to the River Tay,
Most beautiful to be seen,
Near by Dundee and the Magdalen Green.

Beautiful Railway Bridge of the Silvery Tay!
That has caused the Emperor of Brazil to leave
His home far away, *incognito* in his dress,
And view thee ere he passed along *en route*
  to Inverness.

Beautiful Railway Bridge of the Silvery Tay!
The longest of the present day
That has ever crossed o'er a tidal river stream,
Most gigantic to be seen,
Near by Dundee and the Magdalen Green.

Beautiful Railway Bridge of the Silvery Tay!
Which will cause great rejoicing on the opening day,
And hundreds of people will come from far away,
Also the Queen, most gorgeous to be seen,
Near by Dundee and the Magdalen Green.

Beautiful Railway Bridge of the Silvery Tay!
And prosperity to Provost Cox, who has given

Thirty thousand pounds and upwards away
In helping to erect the Bridge of the Tay,
Most handsome to be seen,
Near by Dundee and the Magdalen Green.

Beautiful Railway Bridge of the Silvery Tay!
I hope that God will protect all passengers
By night and by day,
And that no accident will befall them while crossing
The Bridge of the Silvery Tay,
For that would be most awful to be seen
Near by Dundee and the Magdalen Green.

Beautiful Railway Bridge of theSilvery Tay!
And prosperity to Messrs Bouche and Grothe,
The famous engineers of the present day,
Who have succeeded in erecting the Railway
Bridge of the Silvery Tay,
Which stands unequalled to be seen
Near by Dundee and the Magdalen Green.

THE TAY BRIDGE DISASTER

BEAUTIFUL Railway Bridge of the Silv'ry Tay!
Alas! I am very sorry to say
That ninety lives have been taken away
On the last Sabbath day of 1879,
Which will be remember'd for a very long time.

'Twas about seven o'clock at night,
And the wind it blew with all its might,
And the rain came pouring down,

And the dark clouds seem'd to frown,
And the Demon of the air seem'd to say—
"I'll blow down the Bridge of Tay."

When the train left Edinburgh
The passengers' hearts were light and felt no sorrow,
But Boreas blew a terrific gale,
Which made their hearts for to quail,
And many of the passengers with fear did say—
"I hope God will send us safe across the
   Bridge of Tay."

But when the train came near to Wormit Bay,
Boreas he did loud and angry bray,
And shook the central girders of the Bridge of Tay
On the last Sabbath day of 1879,
Which will be remember'd for a very long time.

So the train sped on with all its might,
And Bonnie Dundee soon hove in sight,
And the passengers' hearts felt light,
Thinking they would enjoy themselves on the
   New Year,
With their friends at home they lov'd most dear,
And wish them all a happy New Year.

So the train mov'd slowly along the Bridge of Tay,
Until it was about midway,
Then the central girders with a crash gave way,
And down went the train and passengers into the Tay!

The Storm Field did loudly bray,
Because ninety lives had been taken away,

On the last Sabbath day of 1879,
Which will be remember'd for a very long time.

As soon as the catastrophe came to be known
The alarm from mouth to mouth was blown,
And the cry rang out all o'er the town,
Good Heavens! the Tay Bridge is blown down,
And a passenger train from Edinburgh,
Which fill'd all the people's hearts with sorrow,
And made them for to turn pale,
Because none of the passengers were sav'd to tell
    the tale
How the disaster happen'd on the last Sabbath
    day of 1879,
Which will be remember'd for a very long time.

It must have been an awful sight,
To witness in the dusky moonlight,
While the Storm Fiend did laugh and angry did bray,
Along the Railway Bridge of the Silv'ry Tay.
Oh! ill-fated Bridge of the Silv'ry Tay,
I must now conclude my lay
By telling the world fearlessly without the least
    dismay,
That your central girders would not have given way,
At least many sensible men do say,
Had they been supported on each side with
    buttresses,
At least many a sensible man confesses,
For the stronger we our houses do build,
The less chance we have of being killed.

AN ADDRESS TO THE NEW
TAY BRIDGE

BEAUTIFUL new railway bridge of the Silvery Tay,
With your strong brick piers and buttresses
 in so grand array,
And your thirteen central girders, which seem to
 my eye
Strong enough all windy storms to defy.
And as I gaze upon thee my heart feels gay,
Because thou are the greatest railway bridge
 of the present day,
And can be seen for miles away
From north, south, east, or west of the Tay
On a beautiful and clear sunshiny day,
And ought to make the hearts of the "Mars"
 boys feel gay,
Because thine equal nowhere can be seen,
Only near by Dundee and the bonnie Magdalen Green.

Beautiful new railway bridge of the Silvery Tay,
With thy beautiful side-screens along your railway,
Which will be a great protection on a windy day,
So as the railway carriages won't be blown away,
And ought to cheer the hearts of the passengers
 night and day
As they conveyed along the beautiful railway,
And towering above the Silvery Tay,
Spanning the beautiful river shore to shore
Upwards of two miles or more,
Which is most wonderful to be seen
Near by Dundee and the bonnie Magdalen Green.

Thy structure to my eye seems strong and grand,
And the workmanship most skillfully planned;
And I hope the designers, Messrs Barlow & Arrol,
   will prosper for many a day
For erecting thee across the beautiful Tay.
And I think nobody need have the least dismay
To cross o'er thee by night or by day,
Because thy strength is visible to be seen
Near by Dundee and the bonnie Magdalen Green.

Beautiful new railway bridge of the Silvery Tay,
I wish you success for many a year and a day,
And I hope thousands of people will come from
   far away,
Both high and low without delay,
From the north, south, east, and west,
Because as a railway bridge thou art the best;
Thou standest unequalled to be seen
Near by Dundee and the bonnie Magdalen Green.

And for beauty thou art most lovely to be seen
As the train crosses o'er thee with her cloud of
   steam;
And you look well, painted the colour of marone,
And to find thy equal there is none,
Which, without fear of contradiction,
   I venture to say,
Because you are the longest railway bridge
   of the present day
That now crosses o'er a tidal river stream,
And the most handsome to be seen
Near by Dundee and the bonnie Magdalen Green.

The New Yorkers boast about Brooklyn Bridge
But in comparison to thee it seems like a midge,
Because thou spannest the silvery Tay
A mile or more longer I venture to say;
Besides the railway carriages are pulled across
    by a rope,
Therefore Brooklyn Bridge cannot with thee cope;
And as you have been opened on the 20th day of June,
I hope Her Majesty Queen Victoria will visit
    thee very soon,
Because thou are worthy of a visit from
    Duke, Lord, or Queen,
And strong and securely built, which is most
    worthy to be seen
Near by Dundee and the bonnie Magdalen Green.

A DESCRIPTIVE POEM ON THE
SILVERY TAY

Beautiful silvery Tay,
With your landscapes, so lovely and gay,
Along each side of your waters, to Perth all the way;
No other river in the world has got scenery more fine,
Only I am told the beautiful Rhine,
Near to Wormit Bay, it seems very fine,
Where the Railway Bridge is towering above its
    waters sublime,
And the beautiful ship Mars,
With her Juvenile Tars,
Both lively and gay,
Does carelessly lie

By night and by day,
In the beautiful Bay
Of the silvery Tay.
Beautiful, beautiful! silvery Tay,
Thy scenery is enchanting on a fine summer day,
Near by Balmerino it is beautiful to behold,
When the trees are in full bloom and the cornfields
    seem like gold—
And nature's face seems gay,
And the lambkins they do play,
And the humming bee is on the wing,
It is enough to make one sing,
While they carelessly do stray,
Along the beautiful banks of the silvery Tay,
Beautiful silvery Tay, rolling smoothly on your way,
Near by Newport, as clear as the day,
Thy scenery around is charming I'll be bound ...
And would make the heart of any one feel light
    and gay on a fine summer day,
To view the beautiful scenery along the banks of
    the silvery Tay.

THE FAMOUS TAY WHALE

'Twas in the month of December, and in the year 1883,
That a monster whale came to Dundee,
Resolved for a few days to sport and play,
And devour the small fishes in the silvery Tay.

So the monster whale did sport and play
Among the innocent little fishes in the beautiful Tay,
Until he was seen by some men one day,

And they resolved to catch him without delay.

When it came to be known a whale was seen
   in the Tay,
Some men began to talk and to say,
We must try and catch this monster of a whale.
So come on, brave boys, and never say fail.

Then the people together in crowds did run,
Resolved to capture the whale and to have some fun
So small boats were launched on the silvery Tay,
While the monster of the deep did sport and play.

Oh! it was a most fearful and beautiful sight,
To see it lashing the water with its tail all its might,
And making the water ascend like a shower of hail,
With one lash of its ugly and mighty tail.

Then the water did descend on the men in the boats,
Which wet their trousers and also their coats;
But it only made them the more determined
   to catch the whale,
But the whale shook at them his tail.

Then the whale began to puff and to blow,
While the men and the boats after him did go,
Armed well with harpoons for the fray,
Which they fired at him without dismay.

And they laughed and grinned just like wild baboons,
While they fired at him their sharp harpoons:
But when struck with the harpoons he dived below,
Which filled his pursuers' hearts with woe:

Because they guessed they had lost a prize,
Which caused the tears to well up in their eyes;
And in that their anticipations were only right,
Because he sped on to Stonehaven with all his might:

And was first seen by the crew of the Gourdon
    fishing boat,
Which they thought was a big coble upturned afloat;
But when they drew near they saw it was a whale,
So they resolved to tow it ashore without fail.

So they got a rope from each boat tied round his tail,
And landed their burden at Stonehaven without fail;
And when the people saw it their voices they did raise,
Declaring that the brave fishermen deserved
    great praise.

And my opinion is that God sent the whale in
    time of need,
No matter what other people may think or
    what is their creed;
I know fishermen in general are often very poor,
And God in His goodness sent it drive poverty
    from their door.

So Mr John Wood has bought it for two
    hundred and twenty-six pound,
And has brought it to Dundee all safe and all sound;
Which measures 40 feet in length from the
    snout to the tail,
So I advise the people far and near to see
    it without fail.

Then hurrah! for the mighty monster whale,
Which has got 17 feet 4 inches from tip to tail!
Which can be seen for a sixpence or a shilling,
That is to say, if the people all are willing.

PART III

Most Magnificent to Be Seen

A particularly fecund and coherent department of McGonagall's oeuvre is his topographical poems; they fall into what one might call the "Picture Postcard" mould, which he produced with apparent ease. Apart from having been poetically inspired by the beauty or the history of various places, no doubt the growth in tourism and the Victorian's demand for knowledge of what other places were like played its part in the formation of the following verses.

The Victorian era saw a massive boom in travel, mainly due to the expansion of the railways and the coming of the steam ships. If one looks at a railway map of 1872, then one finds that nearly all of the present main railway lines were already present. Of the great feats of railway engineering in this era, the most notable were the Tay Bridge 1878, the Severn Tunnel 1886 and the Forth Bridge 1890. Striking increases occurred in the volume of traffic on the railways, particularly on the passenger side, in the second half of the reign of Victoria. The increase in population and the extension of route mileage naturally accounted for some of the additional passengers, but there was also the factor of the steady growth of the travel habit. This was nurtured by the railway companies who vied with each other in offering new facilities for the attraction of passengers. Thus in 1872 the Midland, followed by the Great Eastern, announced that it would provide third class travel on all its trains for the low cost of a penny per mile. This bold step paid handsomely, and was largely followed by the other railway companies. Holidays by the seaside "to take the air", or in the country "to take the waters" became a regular part of life of the middle class and even to large sections of the working class. Likewise the concurrent development of the electric telegraph, which came into existence in 1835, made the world a smaller place. With the growth of its domain, news of far-off parts became available almost immediately fostering a desire in many people to know more about foreign places. McGonagall clearly realised this and was suitably "inspired" to provide his audience with the necessary information.

"**Beautiful Edinburgh**" is a tribute to the city of his birth – one of the poems in which McGonagall chose to parade Scotland's capital in front of the rest of the world as one of the finest places on Earth. Clearly Edinburgh was a city majestic enough for a poetic genius to have an affinity for. Having left the city when he was a child, McGonagall was to return as an old man, and was finally to die there. His return to "Modern Athens" was apparently a suitably "grand" occasion. According to newspaper reports, he was met by a few admirers at Waverley Station. When the party reached Princes Street, one of the group ventured to suggest that such a beautiful sight would be worthy of a poem. McGonagall replied, giving one of his characteristically majestic gestures "*I immortalised this scene some years ago*".

In his "**Descriptive Jottings of London**", McGonagall gives us his impressions of the "other" capital city. Following an event in Dundee in which he was duped by an imposter, McGonagall received a generous donation of £5 from the Irish playwrite Dion Boucicault, who obviously felt sorry for him. Having received this money McGonagall decided to visit London to see his benefactor and also the great Victorian actor Henry Irving. It was his belief that they would be able to help him secure a dramatic career on the London stage. According to his spurious "autobiography", written by John Willocks, McGonagall was given a supply of visiting cards by a friend in Dundee to use when calling on people in London, which read thus:

Wm. MCGONAGALL, L. I. A. R. *
Successor to William Shakespeare
Poetry Promptly Executed

*Signifies Lyric Inditer and Reciter

As with most of his travels, the trip to London was to prove a failure. He was stopped from seeing his famous fellow tragedians by the stage doormen of the Lyceum and Adelphi theatres, where Henry Irving and Dion Boucicault were respectively appearing; nor would any of the music halls engage him. Owing to the disappointments he met with, he resolved to return to Dundee, stopping only to see the famous Victorian Baptist preacher C.H. Spurgeon speak at the six thousand seater Metropolitan Tabernacle Hall.

Having travelled around his own country without meeting much success, it was suggested to McGonagall that he could make a fortune if he were prepared to travel to America. He apparently had little trouble in raising the required fare for the passage as friend and foe alike all contributed – the former to oblige him, the latter to rid Dundee of him once and for all. As a generous gesture, the Dundee worthy, and owner of the Temperance Hotel, A.C. Lamb gave him ten shillings and the promise of the return fare should things not work out. Hence, barely six months after the disappointment of his London trip, McGonagall set out on the longest journey of his life– to New York. In March 1877 he sailed from Glasgow in the steerage of the "Circassia" of the Anchor Line. It was a slow boat and took nearly a fortnight to make the crossing. On arriving in New York, McGonagall stayed with a friendly ex-patriot Dundonian, who suggested to him that he should try to secure some theatrical or music hall engagements, before trying his luck selling his broadsheet poetry. Sadly, he could not find anyone willing to engage him and then spent two further fruitless weeks walking the streets of New York trying to peddle his verse. The fact that he was trying to sell broadsheets which had "By Appointment to the Queen" at the top to Republican Americans did not help, but McGonagall was not willing to compromise his allegiance. Eventually, he wired Mr. Lamb for his return fare, and on receipt of same returned home. He wrote the poem "Jottings of New York" on the homeward journey, and the last few stanzas show just how bitter he must have felt towards the city. What starts out optimistically with "...you are wonderful to behold" ends up with the damning comment "One street in Dundee is more worth to me". As the weary Scots traveller's cliché goes "East West Hame's Best !"

In John Willock's account of the poet's life, McGonagall readily admits to not having visited all the subjects of his "Picture Postcards", before having written about them. Returning from New York, he stayed in Glasgow for a month, during which time he gave three private entertainments to crowded audiences and was treated like a Prince. This visit gave him the opportunity to see the sights of Glasgow properly for the first time, and he was greatly impressed. He writes:

"When I began to write uninspired poetry,
as you are aware, I included Glasgow in
the scope of my themes, a proof that my
spirit sometimes wandered west; but when
I wrote that the prettiest river that ever I
saw was Glasgow on the Clyde, it was
merely a poet's licence, and a proof of my
unlimited imagination ....."

Hence, I have selected his poem entitled **"Glasgow"**, which lists all of the major sights, but sadly ends with an unfavourable comparison to his native Edinburgh.

Owing to declining health, and a desire to return "home", McGonagall left Glasgow for Dundee. He had first been visited by the muse in Dundee, and it was always to this Victorian industrial city which his thoughts returned, despite the mockery of many of its inhabitants. The city seems to have tried its best to disassociate itself from this tragic hero ever since he arrived there, but I include here one of his tributes to it – **"Bonnie Dundee in 1878"** – the year he made his fruitless journey to Balmoral. Whilst enjoying one of the most beautiful sites in Europe, Dundee was at that time a smoke filled industrial "Jute City" and it certainly took some of McGonagall's unlimited imagination to call it "Bonnie". His poetry may be a little suspect in quality, but few people have demonstrated as much loyalty to a city in the face of such fierce opposition, as he showed to Dundee.

BEAUTIFUL EDINBURGH

Beautiful city of Edinburgh, most wonderful to be seen,
With your ancient palace of Holyrood and
    Queen's Park Green,
And your big, magnificent, elegant New College,
Where people from all nations can be taught
    knowledge.

The New College of Edinburgh is certainly very grand
Which I consider to be an honour to fair Scotland,
Because it's the biggest in the world, without any doubt,
And is most beautiful in the inside as well as out.

And the Castle is wonderful to look upon,
Which has withstood many angry tempests in
    years bygone;
And the rock it's built upon is rugged and lovely
    to be seen
When the shrubberies surrounding it are blown
    full green.

Morningside is lovely and charming to be seen;
The gardens there are rich with flowers and
    shrubberies green
And sweet scented perfumes fill the air,
Emanating from the sweet flowers and
    beautiful plants there.

And as for Braidhill, it's a very romantic spot,
But a fine place to visit when the weather is hot;
There the air is nice and cool, which will help to
    drive away sorrow

When ye view from its summit the beautiful city
    of Edinburgh.

And as for the statues, they are very grand–
They cannot be surpassed in any foreign land;
And the scenery is attractive and fascinating
    to the eye,
And arrests the attention of tourists as they pass by.

Lord Melville's Monument is most elegant to be seen,
Which is situated in St. Andrew's Square, amongst
    shrubberies green,
Which seems most gorgeous to the eye,
Because it is towering so very high.

The Prince Albert Consort Statue looks very grand,
Especially the granite blocks whereon it doth stand,
Which is admired by all tourists as they pass by,
Because the big granite blocks seem magnificent
    to the eye.

Princes Street West End Garden is fascinating to
    be seen,
With its beautiful big trees and shrubberies green,
And its magnificent water fountain in the valley below
Helps to drive away from the tourist all care and woe.

The Castle Hotel is elegant and grand,
And students visit it from every foreign land,
And the students of Edinburgh often call there
To rest and have luncheon, at a very cheap fare.

Queen Street Garden seems charming to the eye,

And a great boon it is to the tenantry near by,
As they walk along the grand gravel walks near there,
Amongst the big trees and shrubberies,
    and inhale pure air.

Then, all ye tourists, be advised by me,
Beautiful Edinburgh ye ought to go and see.
It's the only city I know of where ye can
    wile away the time
By viewing its lovely scenery and statues fine.

Magnificent city of Edinburgh, I must conclude
    my muse,
But to write in praise of thee I cannot refuse.
I will tell the world boldly without dismay
You have the biggest college in the world at the
    present day.

Of all the cities in the world, Edinburgh for me;
For no matter where I look, some lovely spot I see;
And for picturesque scenery unrivalled you do stand.
Therefore I pronounce you to be the Pride of
    Fair Scotland.

DESCRIPTIVE JOTTINGS OF LONDON

As I stood upon London Bridge and viewed the
    mighty throng
Of thousands of people in cabs and 'busses
    rapidly whirling along,
All furiously driving to and fro,

Up one street and down another as quick as they
     could go:

Then I was struck with the discordant sounds of
     human voices there,
Which seemed to me like wild geese cackling in
     the air:
And the river Thames is a most beautiful sight,
To see the steamers sailing upon it by day and by
     night.

And the Tower of London is most gloomy to behold,
And the crown of England lies there,
     begemmed with precious stones and gold;
King Henry the Sixth was murdered there by the
     Duke of Glo'ster,
And when he killed him with his sword he called
     him an imposter.

St. Paul's Cathedral is the finest building that ever
     I did see,
There's no building can surpass it in the city
     of Dundee,
Because it's magnificent to behold,
With its beautiful dome and spire glittering like gold.

And as for Nelson's Monument that stands in
     Trafalgar Square,
It is a most stately monument I most solemnly
     declare,
And towering defiantly very high,
Which arrests strangers' attention while passing by.

Then there's two beautiful water-fountains
    spouting up very high,
Where the weary traveller can drink when he feels dry;
And at the foot of the monument there's three
    bronze lions in grand array,
Enough to make the stranger's heart throb
    with dismay.

Then there's Mr Spurgeon, a great preacher, which
    no one dare gainsay,
I went to hear him preach on the Sabbath-day,
And he made my heart feel light and gay,
When I heard him preach and pray.

And the Tabernacle was crowded from ceiling to floor,
And many were standing outside the door;
He is an eloquent preacher I honestly declare,
And I was struck with admiration as on him I did stare.

Then there's Petticoat Lane I venture to say,
It's a wonderful place on the Sabbath-day,
There wearing-apparel can be bought to suit the
    young or old.
For the ready cash, silver, coppers, or gold.

Oh! mighty city of London! you are
    wonderful to see,
And thy beauties no doubt fill the tourist's heart
    with glee;
But during my short stay, and while
    wandering there,
Mr Spurgeon was the only man I heard
    speaking proper English I do declare.

JOTTINGS OF NEW YORK
A DESCRIPTIVE POEM

OH mighty City of New York! you are wonderful
    to behold,
Your buildings are magnificent, the truth be it told,
They were the only thing that seemed to arrest my eye,
Because many of them are thirteen storeys high.

And as for Central Park, it is lovely to be seen,
Especially in the summer season when its
    shrubberries and trees are green;
And the Burns' statue is there to be seen,
Surrounded by trees, on the beautiful sward
    so green;
Also, Shakespeare and Sir Walter Scott,
Which by Englishmen and Scotchmen will ne'er
    be forgot.

There the people on the Sabbath-day in
    thousands resort,
All loud in conversation and searching for sport,
Some of them viewing the menagerie of wild
    beasts there,
And also beautiful black swans, I do declare.

And there's beautiful boats to be seen there,
And the joyous shouts of the children do rend the air,
While the boats sail along with them o'er
    Lohengrin Lake,
And the fare is five cents for children and adults
    ten is all they take.

And there's also summer-house shades and merry-
    go-rounds,
And with the merry laughter of the children the
    Park resounds
During the livelong Sabbath-day,
Enjoying the merry-go-round play.

Then there's the elevated railroads, about five
    storeys high,
Which the inhabitants can see and hear night and
    day passing by,
Oh! such a mass of people daily do throng,
No less than five hundred thousand daily pass
    along,
And all along the City you can get for five cents,
And, believe me, among the passengers there are
    few discontent.

And the top of the houses are all flat,
And in the warm weather the people gather
    to chat,
Besides on the house-tops they dry their clothes,
And also many people all night on the housetops
    repose.

And numerous ships and steamboats are there
    to be seen,
Sailing along the East River Water so green;
'Tis certainly a most beautiful sight
To see them sailing o'er the smooth water
    day and night.

And Brooklyn Bridge is a very great height,
And fills the stranger's heart with wonder at first sight,
But with all its loftiness, I venture to say,
For beauty it cannot surpass the new Railway
        Bridge of the Silvery Tay.

And there's also ten thousand rumsellers there,
Oh! wonderful to think, I do declare!
To accommodate the people of that city therein,
And to encourage them to commit all sorts of sin.

And on the Sabbath-day, ye will see many a man
Going for beer with a tin can,
And seems proud to be seen carrying home the beer
To treat his neighbours and family dear.

Then at night numbers of the people dance and sing,
Making the walls of their houses to ring
With their songs and dancing on the Sabbath night,
Which I witnessed with disgust, and fled
        from the sight.

And with regard to New York and the sights
        I did see,
One street in Dundee is more worth to me,
And, believe me, the morning I sailed from
        New York
For Bonnie Dundee, my heart it felt as light
        as a cork.

GLASGOW

BEAUTIFUL city of Glasgow, with your streets so
    neat and clean,
Your stately mansions, and beautiful Green!
Like wise your beautiful bridges across the river Clyde,
And on your bonnie banks I would like to reside.

    Chorus-
Then away to the West– to the beautiful West!
To the fair city of Glasgow that I like the best,
Where the river Clyde rolls on to the sea,
And the lark and the blackbird whistle with glee.

'Tis beautiful to see the ships passing to and fro,
Laden with goods for the high and the low;
So let the beautiful city of Glasgow flourish,
And may the inhabitants always find food
    their bodies to nourish.
    Chorus.

The statue of the Prince of Orange is very grand,
Looking terror to the foe, with a truncheon
    in his hand,
And well mounted on a noble steed, which stands
    in the Trongate,
And holding up its foreleg, I'm sure it looks first rate.
    Chorus.

Then there's the Duke of Wellington's statue in
    Royal Exchange Square–
It is a beautiful statue I without fear declare,
Besides inspiring and most magnificent view,

Because he made the French fly at the battle
    of Waterloo.
    Chorus.

And as for the statue of Sir Walter Scott that stands
    in George Square,
It is a handsome statue – few can with it compare,
And most elegant to be seen,
And close beside it stands the statue of
    Her Majesty the Queen.
    Chorus.

Then there's the statue of Robert Burns in George
    Square,
And the treatment he received when living
    was very unfair;
Now, when he's dead, Scotland's sons for him
    do mourn,
But, alas! unto them he can never return.
    Chorus.

Then as for Kelvin Grove, it is most lovely to be seen
With its beautiful flowers and trees so green,
And a magnificent water-fountain spouting
    up very high,
Where the people can quench their thirst
    when they feel dry.
    Chorus.

Beautiful city of Glasgow, I now conclude
    my muse,
And to write in praise of thee my pen does
    not refuse;

And, without fear of contradiction, I will
    venture to say
You are the second grandest city in Scotland at the
    present day!
    Chorus.

BONNIE DUNDEE IN 1878

Oh, Bonnie Dundee! I will sing in thy praise
A few but true simple lays,
Regarding some of your beauties of the present day—
And virtually speaking, there's none can
    them gainsay;
There's no other town I know of with which you
    can compare
For spinning mills and lasses fair,
And for stately buildings there's none can excel
The beautiful Albert Institute or the Queen's Hotel,
For it is most handsome to be seen,
Where accommodation can be had for Duke,
    Lord or Queen,
And the four pillars of the front are made of
    Aberdeen granite, very fine,
And most beautiful does shine, just like a
    looking glass,
And for beauty and grandeur there's none
    can them surpass.
And your fine shops in Reform Street,
Very few can with them compete
For superfine goods, there's none excel,
From Inverness to Clerkenwell.
And your Tramways, I must confess,

74

That they have proved a complete success,
Which I am right glad to see ...
And a very great improvement to Bonnie Dundee.
And there's the Royal Arch, most handsome
    to be seen,
Erected to the memory of our Most Gracious Queen—
Most magnificent to see,
And a very great honour to the people of Dundee.
Then there's the Baxter Park, most beautiful
    to see,
And a great boon it is to the people of Dundee,
For there they can enjoy themselves when
    they are free from care,
By inhaling the perfumed air,
Emanating from the sweet flowers and green trees
    and shrubs there.
Oh, Bonnie Dundee! I must conclude my muse,
And to write in praise of thee, my pen does
    not refuse,
Your beauties that I have alluded to are most
    worthy to see,
And in conclusion, I will call thee Bonnie Dundee!

PART IV

It was a Most Solemn Sight to See

In all of his poems, McGonagall shows a reverance for, and devotion to, an idea of "Greatness". This is perhaps most typically displayed when he writes about Kings and Queens; however, when none were available, he found inspiration from the "greatness" of lesser grandees such as Princes, Dukes, Generals, Philanthropists, and local worthies. For McGonagall, with his sense of the dramatic, this "greatness" became even more inspiring when it could be associated with death or disaster. In his youth he had spent most of his spare time reading, and his favourite reading matter was Shakespeare's plays especially Macbeth, Richard III, Hamlet and Othello. Hence one might crudely attribute at least some of his later relish in the death of kings and other large scale disasters to the subject matter of these early influences.

It must also be noted that in Victorian Britain, death, dying and bereavement became highly defined social rituals almost attaining the status of art forms. In the nineteenth century, mourning and widowhood, at least for those who could afford it, were governed by strict social conventions. Even in the cases where people were married to unfaithful or unloveable spouses, a convincing show of grief was still expected when they died. When the deceased was a close relation or friend, death became a fetish to be worshipped with accepted rites. These attitudes to death were further magnified when, in 1861, the Queen's husband Prince Albert died. She wrote "My life as a happy one is ended! The world has gone for me". Somehow her own sense of deep loss pervaded society and death and bereavement became subjects worthy of writing poetry about, more than ever before. Following in the traditions of earlier folk poets, McGonagall did just this, penning many lines about the deaths or funerals of contemporary notables.

This section begins with perhaps McGonagall's best known poem of this genre – **"The Death of Lord and Lady Dalhousie"**. Sir John William Ramsay became the thirteenth Earl of Dalhousie in 1880. His early career was in the Navy which he joined in 1861. During his period of service he married Lady Louisa Bennett in 1877 before finally retiring in 1879 to devote himself to academic study and politics. He became the Liberal M.P. for Liverpool in 1880, before being created the Secretary for Scotland in 1886. The Earl and Countess were said to have been an ideally happy couple, and were held in high regard by their Forfarshire tenants. In the poem, McGonagall expresses a wish for the people to build a monument to the couple. Such a monument was built later that very year, and still stands today, for it is through the famous "Dalhousie Arch" that visitors from the south enter the town of Edzell.

It is not surprising that McGonagall should have written about **"The Burial of the Rev. George Gilfillan"** for he was the subject of his very first poem, and encouraged McGonagall to write. Gilfillan was a much respected orator, preacher and local benefactor in Dundee. The poet was often seen around Dundee wearing an old frock coat which is said to have been given to him by this divine benefactor. An account from John Willocks provides us with an interesting picture of McGonagall in attendance at the aforementioned funeral:–

"At the funeral of George Gilfillan, one of the largest ever held in Dundee, the 'poet' appeared in an almost indescribable character costume of red, whether it was the Royal Stuart tartan or Rob Roy or a Roman toga, has never been defined; in his hand a huge scroll and his spindle shanks encased in flesh-coloured tights. But for the solemn occasion the 'poet' would certainly have fallen prey to the non-gloved hands of the Dundee youth of the period and been ducked in the horse trough."

William Ewart Gladstone (1809-1898), as well as being a Liberal statesman, was Prime Minister of Great Britain (1868-74, 1880-85, 1886, 1892-94) during a great part of McGonagall's poetic career. Originally a Conservative, Gladstone became a leader of the Liberal Party in 1867 and soon afterwards served his first term as Prime Minister. He disestablished and disendowed the Irish Church, and established a system of national education in 1870. As one of the major figures of the Victorian age, McGonagall had to write about **"The Burial of Mr. Gladstone"**, for in the poets words Gladstone was "The *greatest* politician of his day". The poem is crammed brimful with the names of famous mourners who attended the funeral. No doubt as well as worshipping at the altar of "Greatness", the penniless McGonagall was also conscious of the audience of potential patrons who might like the idea of being immortalised in verse. This piece reads like something akin to a modern day gossip column.

With **"The Death of Prince Leopold"** we see one of McGonagall's Royal Laments, this time for Queen Victoria's favourite son. Prince Leopold was born on 7th April 1853, and was from the outset an ailing baby – later it was discovered that he suffered from haemophilia. Although his health had made him the most difficult of the children for the Queen to bring up, it also created a very strong and special bond between the two. Prince Leopold married Princess Helen of Waldbeck in 1882, although the Queen is reported to have been saddened that the bridegroom was still "lame and shakey". He died in 1884, and the sense of loss of her favourite son was so great that Queen Victoria wrote in her journal "I am a poor desolate old woman, and my cup of sorrow overflows". As usual, McGonagall gives us a full descriptive account of the "grand" funeral proceedings which he must have gleaned from newspaper reports of the time.

"**The Tragic Death of the Reverend A.H. Mackonochie**" brings to a close this somewhat sombre section. Alexander Heriot Mackonochie (1825-87) was a famous Victorian divine from Wadham College Oxford, who adopted advanced ritualistic views, and was subjected to a series of lawsuits promoted by the Church Association between 1867 and 1882. As with many of his "tragic" poems, this one is so full of bathos that one is more likely to be left with a smile on ones face than a tear in the eye.

DEATH OF LORD AND LADY
DALHOUSIE

ALAS! Lord and Lady Dalhousie are dead, and
    buried at last,
Which causes many people to feel a little downcast;
And both lie side by side in one grave,
But I hope God in His goodness their souls will save.

And may He protect their children that are
    left behind,
And may they always food and raiment find;
And from the paths of virtue may they ne'er be led,
And may they always find a house wherein to lay
    their head.

Lord Dalhousie was a man worthy of all praise,
And to his memory I hope a monument the people
    will raise,
That will stand for many ages to come
To commemorate the good deeds he has done.

He was beloved by men of high and low degree,
Especially in Forfarshire by his tenantry:
And by many of the inhabitants in and around Dundee,
Because he was affable in temper, and void of all vanity.

He had great affection for his children, also his wife,
'Tis said he loved her as dear as his life;
And I trust they are now in heaven above,
Where all is joy, peace, and love.

At the age of fourteen he resolved to go to sea,

So he entered the training ship Britannia belonging
    to the navy,
And entered as a midshipman as he considered
    most fit
Then passed through the course of training with the
    greatest credit.

In a short time he obtained the rank of lieutenant,
Then to her Majesty's ship Galatea he was sent;
Which was under the command of the Duke
    of Edinburgh,
And during his service there he felt but little sorrow.

And from that he was promoted to be commander
    of the Britannia,
And was well liked by the men, for what he said
    was law;
And by him Prince Albert Victor and Prince
    George received a naval education.
Which met with the Prince of Wales' most hearty
    approbation.

'Twas in the year 1877 he married the Lady Ada
    Louisa Bennett,
And by marrying that noble lady he ne'er did regret;
And he was ever ready to give his service in any way,
Most willingly and cheerfully by night or by day.

'Twas in the year of 1887, and on Thursday the
    1st of December,
Which his relatives and friends will long remember
That were present at the funeral in Cockpen
    churchyard,

Because they had for the noble Lord a great regard.

About eleven o'clock the remains reached Dalhousie,
And were met by a body of the tenantry;
They conveyed them inside the building,
    all seemingly woe-begone,
And among those that sent wreaths was Lord
    Claude Hamilton.

Those that sent wreaths were but very few,
But one in particular was the Duke of Buccleuch;
Besides Dr. Herbert Spencer, and Countess
    Rosebery, and Lady Bennett,
Which no doubt were sent by them with heartfelt
    regret.

Besides those that sent wreaths in addition were
    the Earl and Countess of Aberdeen,
Especially the Prince of Wales' was most lovely to
    be seen,
And the Earl of Dalkeith's wreath was very pretty too,
With a mixture of green and white flowers,
    beautiful to view.

Amongst those present at the interment were
    Mr Marjoribanks, M.P.,
Also ex-Provost Ballingall from Bonnie Dundee;
Besides the Honourable W. G. Colville, representing
    the Duke and Duchess of Edinburgh,
While in every one's face standing at the grave
    was depicted sorrow.

The funeral service was conducted in the Church
          of Cockpen
By the Rev. J. Crabb, of St. Andrew's
          Episcopal Church, town of Brechin;
And as the two coffins were lowered into
          their last resting-place,
Then the people retired with sad hearts at a quick pace.

THE BURIAL OF THE REV. GEORGE GILFILLAN

ON the Gilfillan burial day,
In the Hill o' Balgay,
It was a most solemn sight to see,
Not fewer than thirty thousand people
          assembled in Dundee,
All watching the funeral procession of Gilfillan
          that day,
That death had suddenly taken away,
And was going to be buried in the Hill o' Balgay.
There were about three thousand people in
          the procession alone,
And many were shedding tears, and several did
          moan,
And their bosoms heaved with pain,
Because they knew they would never look upon
          his like again.
There could not be fewer than fifty carriages
          in the procession that day,
And gentlemen in some of them that had
          come from far away,
And in whispers some of them did say,
As the hearse bore the precious corpse away,

Along the Nethergate that day.
I'm sure he will be greatly missed by the poor,
For he never turned them empty-handed away
        from his door;
And to assist them in distress it didn't give him pain,
And I'm sure the poor will never look upon
        his like again.
On the Gilfillan burial day, in the Hill o' Balgay,
There was a body of policemen marshalled in
        grand array,
And marched in front of the procession all the way;
Also the relatives and friends of the deceas'd,
Whom I hope from all sorrows has been releas'd,
And whose soul I hope to heaven has fled away,
To sing with saints above for ever and aye.
The Provost, Magistrates, and Town Council were
        in the procession that day;
Also Mrs Gilfillan, who cried and sobbed all
        the way
For her kind husband, that was always affable
        and gay,
Which she will remember until her dying day.
When the procession arrived in the Hill o' Balgay,
The people were almost as hush as death, and
        many of them did say–
As long as we live we'll remember the day
That the great Gilfillan was buried in the
        Hill o' Balgay.
When the body of the great Gilfillan was lowered
        into the grave,
'Twas then the people's hearts with sorrow did heave;
And with tearful eyes and bated breath,
Mrs Gilfillan lamented her loving husband's death.

Then she dropped a ringlet of immortelles
        into his grave,
Then took one last fond look, and in sorrow did leave;
And all the people left with sad hearts that day,
And that ended the Gilfillan burial in the
        Hill o' Balgay.

THE BURIAL OF MR. GLADSTONE
THE GREAT POLITICAL HERO

Alas! the people now do sigh and moan
For the loss of Wm. Ewart Gladstone,
Who was a very great politician and a moral man,
And to gainsay it there's few people can.

'Twas in the year of 1898, and on the 19th of May,
When his soul took its flight for ever and aye,
And his body lies interred in Westminster Abbey;
But I hope his soul has gone to that Heavenly shore,
Where all trials and troubles cease for evermore.

He was a man of great intellect and genius bright,
And ever faithful to his Queen by day and by night,
And always foremost in a political fight;
And for his services to mankind, God will
        him requite.

The funeral procession was affecting to see,
Thousands of people were assembled there,
        of every degree;
And it was almost eleven o'clock when the
        procession left Westminster Hall,

And the friends of the deceased were present–
      physicians and all.

A large force of police was also present there,
And in the faces of the spectators there was a pitiful air,
Yet they were orderly in every way,
And newspaper boys were selling publications
      without delay.

Present in the procession was Lord Playfair,
And Bailie Walcot was also there,
Also Mr Macpherson of Edinboro–
And all seemingly to be in profound sorrow.

The supporters of the coffin were the Earl Rosebery,
And the Right Honourable Earl of Kimberley,
And the Right Honourable Sir W. Vernon he was there,
And his Royal Highness the Duke of York,
      I do declare.

George Armitstead, Esq., was there also,
And Lord Rendal, with his heart full of woe;
And the Right Honourable Duke of Rutland,
And the Right Honourable Arthur J. Balfour, on
      the right hand;
Likewise the noble Marquis of Salisbury,
And His Royal Highness the Prince of Wales,
      of high degree.

And immediately behind the coffin was Lord
      Pembroke,
The representative of Her Majesty, and the Duke
      of Norfolk,

Carrying aloft a beautiful short wand,
The insignia of his high, courtly office, which
      looked very grand.

And when the procession arrived at the grave,
      Mrs Gladstone was there,
And in her countenance was depicted a very grave air;
And the dear, good lady seemed to sigh and moan
For her departed, loving husband,
      Wm. Ewart Gladstone.

And on the opposite side of her stood
      Lord Pembroke,
And Lord Salisbury, who wore a skull cap and cloak;
Also the Prince of Wales and the Duke of Rutland,
And Mr Balfour and Lord Spencer,
      all looking very bland.

And the clergy were gathered about the head
      of the grave,
And the attention of the spectators the Dean did crave;
Then he said, "Man that is born of woman
      hath a short time to live,
But, Oh, Heavenly Father! do thou our sins forgive."

Then Mrs Gladstone and her two sons knelt down
      by the grave,
Then the Dean did the Lord's blessing crave,
While Mrs Gladstone and her sons knelt,
While the spectators for them great pity felt.

The scene was very touching and profound,
To see all the mourners bending their heads

to the ground,
And, after a minute's most silent prayer,
The leave-taking at the grave was affecting,
I do declare.

Then Mrs Gladstone called on little Dorothy Drew,
And immediately the little girl to her grandmamma flew,
And they both left the grave with their heads
bowed down,
While tears from their relatives fell to the ground.

Immortal Wm. Ewart Gladstone! I must conclude
my muse,
And to write in praise of thee my pen does not refuse—
To tell the world, fearlessly, without the least dismay,
You were the greatest politician in your day.

THE DEATH OF PRINCE LEOPOLD

ALAS! noble Prince Leopold, he is dead!
Who often has his lustre shed:
Especially by singing for the benefit of
Esher School,—
Which proves he was a wise prince, and no
conceited fool.

Methinks I see him on the platform singing
the *Sands o' Dee*,
The generous-hearted Leopold, the good and the free,
Who was manly in his actions, and beloved
by his mother;
And in all the family she hasn't got such another.

He was of a delicate constitution all his life,
And he was his mother's favourite, and very kind
        to his wife,
And he had also a particular liking for his child,
And in his behaviour he was very mild.

Oh! noble-hearted Leopold, most beautiful to see,
Who was wont to fill your audience's hearts
        with glee,
With your charming songs, and lectures against
        strong drink:
Britain had nothing else to fear, as far as you
        could think.

A wise prince you were, and well worthy of the name,
And to write in praise of thee I cannot refrain;
Because you were ever ready to defend that
        which is right,
Both pleasing and righteous in God's eye-sight.

And for the loss of such a prince the people will mourn,
But, alas! unto them he can never more return,
Because sorrow never could revive the dead again,
Therefore to weep for him is all in vain.

'Twas on Saturday the 12th of April, in the year 1884,
He was buried in the royal vault, never to rise more
Until the last trump shall sound to summon him away.

When the Duchess of Albany arrived she drove
        through the Royal Arch,—
A little before the Seaforth Highlanders set
        out on the funeral march;

And she was received with every sympathetic respect,
Which none of the people present seem'd to neglect.

Then she entered the memorial chapel and stayed
        a short time
And as she viewed her husband's remains it was
        really sublime,
While her tears fell fast on the coffin lid without delay,
Then she took one last fond look, and hurried away.

At half-past ten o'clock the Seaforth Highlanders
        did appear,
And every man in the detachment his medals did wear;
And they carried their side-arms by their side,
With mournful looks, but full of love and pride.

Then came the Coldstream Guards headed
        by their band,
Which made the scene appear imposing and grand;
Then the musicians drew up in front of the guardroom,
And waited patiently to see the prince laid in the
        royal tomb.

First in the procession were the servants of
        His late Royal Highness,
And next came the servants of the Queen in deep
        mourning dress,
And the gentlemen of his household in deep distress,
Also General Du Pla, who accompanied the
        remains from Cannes.

The coffin was borne by eight Highlanders of his
        own regiment,

And the fellows seemed to be rather discontent
For the loss of the prince they loved most dear,
While adown their cheeks stole many a silent tear.

Then behind the corpse came the Prince of Wales
          in field marshal uniform,
Looking very pale, dejected, careworn, and forlorn;
Then followed great magnates, all dressed in uniform,
And last, but not least, the noble Marquis of Lorne.

The scene in George's Chapel was most
          magnificent to behold,
The banners of the knights of the garter
          embroidered with gold;
Then again it was most touching and lovely to see
The Seaforth Highlanders' inscription to the
          Prince's memory:

It was wrought in violets, upon a background of
          white flowers,
And as they gazed upon it their tears fell in showers;
But the whole assembly were hushed when Her
          Majesty did appear,
Attired in her deepest mourning, and from her eye
          there fell a tear.

Her Majesty was unable to stand long, she
          was overcome with grieff,
And when the Highlanders lowered the coffin into
          the tomb she felt relief;
Then the ceremony closed with singing
          "Lead, kindly light,"

Then the Queen withdrew in haste from the
        mournful sight.

Then the Seaforth Highlanders' band played
        "Lochaber no more,"
While the brave soldiers' hearts felt depressed and sore;
And as homeward they marched they let fall many a tear
For the loss of the virtues Prince Leopold they
        loved so dear.

THE TRAGIC DEATH OF
THE REV. A.H. MACKONOCHIE

FRIENDS of humanity, of high and low degree,
I pray ye all come listen to me;
And truly I will relate to ye,
The tragic fate of the Rev. Alexander Heriot
        Mackonochie.

Who was on a visit to the Bishop of Argyle,
For the good of his health, for a short while;
Because for the last three years his memory had
        been affected,
Which prevented him from getting his thoughts
        collected.

'Twas on Thursday, the 15th of December,
        in the year of 1887,
He left the Bishop's house to go and see Loch Leven;
And he was accompanied by a little Skye terrier
        and a deer-hound,
Besides the Bishop's two dogs, that knew
        well the ground.

And as he had taken the same walk the day before,
The Bishop's mind was undisturbed and easy
             on that score;
Besides the Bishop had been told by some men,
That they saw him making his way up a glen.

From which a river flows down with a mighty roar,
From the great mountains of the Mamore;
And this route led him towards trackless
                wastes eastward,
And no doubt to save his life he had
             struggled very hard.

And as Mr Mackonochie had not returned
             at dinner time,
The Bishop ordered two men to search for him,
             which they didn't decline;
Then they searched for him along the road he
             should have returned,
But when they found him not, they sadly mourned.

And when the Bishop heard it, he procured a
             carriage and pair,
While his heart was full of woe, and in a state of despair;
He organised three search parties without delay,
And headed one of the parties in person
             without dismay.

And each party searched in a different way,
But to their regret at the end of the day;
Most unfortunately no discovery had been made,
Then they lost hope of finding him, and began to
             be afraid.

And as a last hope, two night searches were planned,
And each party with well lighted lamps in hand
Started on their perilous mission, Mr Mackonochie
        to try and find,
In the midst of driving hail, and the howling wind.

One party searched a distant sporting lodge with
        right good will,
Besides through brier, and bush, and snow, on the hill;
And the Bishop's party explored the Devil's
        Staircase with hearts full of woe,
A steep pass between the Kinloch hills,
        and the hills of Glencoe.

Oh! it was a pitch dark and tempestuous night,
And the searchers would have lost their way
        without lamp light;
But the brave searchers stumbled along for hours,
        but slow,
Over rocks, and ice, and sometimes through deep snow.

And as the Bishop's party were searching they met
        a third party from Glencoe side,
Who had searched bracken and burn, and the
        country wide;
And sorrow was depicted in each one's face,
Because of the Rev. Mr Mackonochie they could
        get no trace.

But on Saturday morning the Bishop set off again,
Hoping that the last search wouldn't prove in vain;
Accompanied with a crowd of men and dogs,
All resolved to search the forest and the bogs.

And the party searched with might and main,
Until they began to think their search would
            prove in vain;
When the Bishop's faithful dogs raised a pitiful cry,
Which was heard by the searchers near by.

Then the party pressed on right manfully,
And sure enough there were the dogs guarding
            the body of Mackonochie;
And the corpse was cold and stiff, having
            been long dead,
Alas! almost frozen, and a wreath of snow
            around the head.

And as the searchers gathered round the body in
            pity they did stare,
Because his right foot was stained with blood, and bare;
But when the Bishop o'er the corpse had
            offered up a prayer,
He ordered his party to carry the corpse to his
            house on a bier.

So a bier of sticks was most willingly and
            quickly made,
Then the body was tenderly upon it laid;
And they bore the corpse and laid inside the
            Bishop's private chapel,
Then the party took one sorrowful look and bade
            the corpse farewell.

PART V

But Accidents will happen by
Land and the Sea

The theme of "Accidents" brings together the strands of
some of the strongest influences on McGonagall's poetry
– his Scots–Irish legacy from the folk poets, his sense of,
and ability to deliver, the "dramatic", and the Victorian
preoccupation with death and disaster.

Accidents were always a popular subject for folk
poets, who not only relished a dramatic narrative and heart
rending subject which would draw a crowd, but also saw
it as their purpose to carry oral history to the illiterate
masses. The Victorians seemed morbidly fascinated by
disasters, partially because of their desire to wallow in
grief, and also because of their desire to find or create
heroes and heroines who could be held up as shining moral
examples to others.

Undoubtably McGonagall's most famous work con-
cerning an accident is "The Tay Bridge Disaster". I have
included it elsewhere in this book, so begin this section
with another prime example of this genre - "Grace
Darling; or the Wreck of the 'Forfarshire'". Here
McGonagall gives an historical report of a dramatic event
which not only includes tales of heroism, but also a local
link for his Dundee audience. They may have been disas-
ters involving greater loss of life and ones which included
braver actions by persons involved, however the heroic
act of the young English girl Grace Darling became a
classic Victorian tale. The steamship "Forfarshire" was
built at Adamsons' yard in Dundee, and was launched on

the 5th December 1835. At that time she was the largest steamer constructed in a Dundee yard, and a huge crowd gathered to witness the launch. The ship was specially designed as a passenger steamer to be introduced on the Dundee to Hull route. In May of 1836 the "Forfarshire" made her first voyage to Hull, oustripping the "Perth" – then the fastest steamer on the route – and soon became the favourite. However the career of the ship was to be brief as disaster was to befall it only two years and four months later.

On Saturday the 1st September 1838 the "Forfarshire" sailed safely from Dundee to Hull. She left to make the return journey on Wednesday 5th September, but was fated never to enter the Tay again. The steamer ran aground on Harker's Rock, about half a mile from the Longstone Lighthouse on the furthermost of the Farne Islands. The keeper of the lighthouse was William Darling who lived there with his wife and one daughter – Grace Darling. When the disaster struck, father and daughter rowed out to the stricken ship, in almost impossible seas, and found five men clinging to a rock in the wild sea; they then managed to bring the men onto the lifeboat. Both William and his daughter Grace received gold medals for bravery from the Humane Society for their heroism. Grace Darling's place in the Victorian public's heart was further bolstered by her tragic death from consumption barely three years later. What better subject could McGonagall hope to find for a dramatic epic poem?

In his poem **"The Wreck of the Steamer 'London', while on her way to Australia"**, McGonagall obviously delights in trying to heighten the drama and intensify the tragedy by relating the fateful tale of one of its passengers Gustavus V. Brooke. Clearly he was a tragic hero with

98

whom the poet felt some affinity. Gustavus Vaughan Brooke was a famous Victorian actor of Irish extraction who toured England and Scotland calling himself the "Dublin Roscius". He is said to have had a good presence on stage and a fine voice, however intemperance led to a chequered career during which he alternately triumphed and failed in such Shakespearian roles as Richard III, Othello and Hamlet. It is hardly surprising that McGonagall should identify with such a character who clearly appealed to his sense of romance. Brooke worked in London, America and Australia, but was finally imprisoned for debt in Warwick jail. Bar the intemperance, McGonagall obviously saw himself as a kindred spirit – the broken actor who did not receive his just rewards from a cruel and unappreciative world. On his release, Brooke set sail for Australia, but was drowned when his ship sank in the Bay of Biscay accident which McGonagall relates in this poem. Reading the poem one gets the feeling that to McGonagall, no finer end could befall a great actor than to finally play out his last roll in the tragedy which brings about his own demise.

The final sea-borne accident which I include here is an historical poem about **"The Wreck of the Whaler 'Oscar'"**.

This story of shipwreck had probably entered the folk lore of the North East of Scotland by the time McGonagall chose to write about it, for cities such as Aberdeen and Dundee were home to Britain's whaling fleet. Ships sailed from the North East every year to hunt whales in the Arctic waters of the Davis Straits and Greenland. Blubber was used in the manufacture of oil and the smell of whale oil would have been familiar to McGonagall. The incident which McGonagall relates with his customary attention to detail took place in 1813. After a spell of fine weather, five whalers were riding at anchor, prior to heading for the arctic hunting grounds, when the weather abruptly deteriorated. Two of them, the "St. Andrews" and the "Oscar" weighed anchor and tried to stand out to sea to clear Girdle Ness promontary, when the wind fell light and both were carried inshore by the tide. They both had to drop anchor again, however the winds abruptly strengthened again, rapidly rising to a gale. The "St. Andrews" being slightly further out cut both of its cables and just managed to weather Girdle Ness. Tragically the "Oscar" was too close inshore and was drive on to the rocks of Greyhope Bay, where she immediately started to break up. The forecastle was the last section of the hull to remain above water and the ships master, Captain Innes, and five of his crew found a brief refuge there before disappearing into the sea. Of a crew of 44 men only two survived.

The landbased accidents which McGonagall wrote about were usually reports of horrific fires, and the poems which follow are no exceptions. Both of these pieces exemplify McGonagall's use of contemporary events as dramatic subjects for his "journalistic" poems. In these poems he always reports the tragedies in detail, using the names of known participants whenever possible to heighten the sense of personal loss and grief involved. Here we find the Victorian public's demand for news and the folk poet's desire to immortalise a dramatic event fusing to create poetic journalism.

"The Clepington Catastrophe" provides us with an account of a disastrous fire in a Jute Store. In Dundee such fires were not uncommon, and in 1835 the Town Council had been forced to form its own primitive Fire Brigade, which over the years became all too familiar with the which over the years became all too familiar with the highly dangerous nature of fires in jute warehouses. On this occasion, McGonagall informs us the fire claimed the lives of four men.

"The Burning of the People's Variety Theatre, Aberdeen" is another harrowing report of human tragedy and loss of life. In Victorian times safety standards in public buildings were not as high as they are nowadays. With the advent in 1833 of the lucifer match, the use of gas lighting in theatres, and the general overcrowding of public arenas, it is hardly surprising that such calamities occurred.

Whilst the poems which follow are as amusing as anything else which McGonagall wrote (perhaps more amusing because one is aware of how serious they are supposed to be), one must remember that they would have seemed far more stirring when performed by the author himself. He was a fine orator, and it is perhaps wrong to divorce the poems from their performance, for McGonagall was after all a "Poet and tragedian".

GRACE DARLING
OR
THE WRECK OF THE "FORFARSHIRE"

As the night was beginning to close in one rough
       September day
In the year of 1838, a steamer passed through the
       Fairway
Between the Farne Islands and the coast, on her
       passage northwards;
But the wind was against her, and the steamer
       laboured hard.

There she laboured in the heavy sea against both
       wind and tide,
Whilst a dense fog enveloped her on every side;
And the mighty billows made her timbers creak,
Until at last, unfortunately, she sprung a leak.

Then all hands rushed to the pumps, and wrought
       with might and main.
But the water, alas! alarming on them did gain;
And the thick sleet was driving across the raging sea,
While the wind it burst upon them in all its fury.

And the fearful gale and the murky aspect of the sky
Caused the passengers on board to lament and sigh
As the sleet drove thick, furious, and fast,
And as the waves surged mountains high,
       they stood aghast.

And the screaming of the sea-birds foretold a
       gathering storm,

And the passengers, poor souls, looked pale and forlorn,
And on every countenance was depicted woe
As the "Forfarshire" steamer was pitched to and fro.

And the engine-fires with the water were washed out;
Then, as the tide set strongly in, it wheeled
      the vessel about,
And the ill-fated vessel drifted helplessly along;
But the fog cleared up a little as the night wore on.

Then the terror-stricken crew saw the breakers ahead,
And all thought of being saved from them fled;
And the Farne lights were shining hazily through
      the gloom,
While in the fore-cabin a woman lay with two
      children in a swoon.

Before the morning broke, the "Forfarshire" struck
      upon a rock,
And was dashed to pieces by a tempestuous shock,
Which raised her for a moment, and dashed her
      down again,
Then the ill-starred vessel was swallowed up in the
      briny main.

Before the vessel broke up, some nine or ten
      of the crew intent
To save their lives, or perish in the attempt,
Lowered one of the boats while exhausted and forlorn,
And, poor souls, were soon lost sight of in the storm.

Around the windlass on the forecastle some dozen
      poor wretches clung,

And with despair and grief their weakly hearts
        were rung
As the merciless sea broke o'er them every moment;
But God in His mercy to them Grace Darling sent.

By the first streak of dawn she early up had been,
And happened to look out upon the stormy scene,
And she descried the wreck through the morning gloom;
But she resolved to rescue them from such a
        perilous doom.

Then she cried, Oh! father dear, come here
        and see the wreck,
See, here take the telescope, and you can inspect;
Oh! father, try and save them, and heaven
        will you bless;
But, my darling, no help can reach them in such a
        storm as this.

Oh! my kind father, you will surely try and save
These poor souls from a cold and watery grave;
Oh! I cannot sit to see them perish before mine eyes,
And, for the love of heaven, do not my pleading despise!

Then old Darling yielded, and launched the little boat,
And high on the big waves the boat did float;
Then Grace and her father took each an oar in hand,
And to see Grace Darling rowing the picture was grand.

And as the little boat to the sufferers drew near,
Poor souls, they tried to raise a cheer;
But as they gazed upon the heroic Grace,
The big tears trickled down each sufferer's face.

And nine persons were rescued almost dead
        with the cold
By modest and lovely Grace Darling, that heroine bold;
The survivors were taken to the light-house, and
        remained there two days,
And every one of them was loud in Grace
        Darling's praise.
Grace Darling was a comely lass, with long, fair
        floating hair,
With soft blue eyes, and shy, and modest rare;
And her countenance was full of sense and
        genuine kindliness,
With a noble heart, and ready to help suffering
        creatures in distress.

But, alas! three years after her famous exploit,
Which, to the end of time, will never be forgot,
Consumption, that fell destroyer, carried her away
To heaven, I hope, to be an angel for ever and aye.

Before she died, scores of suitors in marriage
        sought her hand;
But no, she'd rather live in Longstone light-house
        on Farne island,
And there she lived and died with her father
        and mother,
And for her equal in true heroism we cannot
        find another.

THE WRECK OF THE STEAMER "LONDON"
WHILE ON HER WAY TO AUSTRALIA

'TWAS in the year of 1866, and on a very
      beautiful day,
That eighty-two passengers, with spirits light and gay,
Left Gravesend harbour, and sailed gaily away
On board the steamship "London,"
Bound for the city of Melbourne,
Which unfortunately was her last run,
Because she was wrecked on the stormy main,
Which has caused many a heart to throb with pain,
Because they will ne'er look upon their lost ones again.

'Twas on the 11th of January they anchored
      at the Nore;
The weather was charming– the like was seldom
      seen before,
Especially the next morning as they came in sight
Of the charming and beautiful Isle of Wight,
But the wind it blew a terrific gale towards night,
Which caused the passengers' hearts to shake
      with fright,
And caused many of them to sigh and mourn,
And whisper to themselves, we will ne'er
      see Melbourne.

Amongst the passengers was Gustavus V. Brooke,
Who was to be seen walking on the poop,
Also clergymen, and bankers, and magistrates also,
All chatting merrily together in the cabin below;
And also wealthy families returning to their dear
      native land,

And accomplished young ladies, most lovely and grand,
All in the beauty and bloom of their pride,
And some with their husbands sitting close by their side.

'Twas all on a sudden the storm did arise,
Which took the captain and passengers all by surprise,
Because they had just sat down to their tea,
When the ship began to roll with the heaving of the sea,
And shipped a deal of water, which came down
        on their heads,
Which wet their clothes and also their beds;
And caused a fearful scene of consternation,
And amongst the ladies great tribulation,
And made them cry out, Lord, save us from
        being drowned,
And for a few minutes the silence was profound.

Then the passengers began to run to and fro,
With buckets to bale out the water between decks below,
And Gustavus Brooke quickly leapt from his bed
In his Garibaldi jacket and drawers, without
        fear or dread,
And rushed to the pump, and wrought with
        might and main;
But alas! all their struggling was in vain,
For the water did fast on them gain;
But he enacted a tragic part until the last,
And sank exhausted when all succour was past;
While the big billows did lash her o'er,
And the Storm-fiend did laugh and roar.

Oh, Heaven! it must have really been
A most harrowing and pitiful scene

To hear mothers and their children loudly screaming,
And to see the tears adown their pale faces streaming,
And to see a clergyman engaged in prayer,
Imploring God their lives to spare,
Whilst the cries of the women and children
      did rend the air.

Then the captain cried, Lower down the small boats,
And see if either of them sinks or floats;
Then the small boats were launched on the
      stormy wave,
And each one tried hard his life to save
From a merciless watery grave.

A beautiul young lady did madly cry and rave,
"Five hundred sovereigns, my life to save!"
But she was by the sailors plainly told
For to keep her filthy gold,
Because they were afraid to overload the boat,
Therefore she might either sink or float,
Then went down with the ship to the bottom
      of the sea,
Along with Gustavus Brooke, who was wont to fill
      our hearts with glee
While performing Shakespearian tragedy.

And out of eight-two passengers only twenty
      were saved,
And that twenty survivors most heroically behaved.
For three stormy days and stormy nights they were
      tossed to and fro
On the raging billows, with their hearts full of woe,
Alas! poor souls, not knowing where to go,

Until at last they all agreed to steer for the south,
And they chanced to meet an Italian barque bound
for Falmouth,
And they were all rescued from a watery grave,
And they thanked God and Captain Cavassa, who
did their lives save.

THE WRECK OF THE WHALER "OSCAR"

'TWAS on the 1st of April, and in the year of
Eighteen thirteen,
That the whaler "Oscar" was wrecked not far
from Aberdeen;
'Twas all on a sudden the wind arose, and a
terrific blast it blew,
And the "Oscar" was lost, and forty-two of a
gallant crew.

The storm burst forth with great violence, but
of short duration,
And spread o'er a wide district, and filled the
people's hearts with consternation,
And its effects were such that the people will
long mind,
Because at Peterhead the roof was torn off a
church by the heavy wind.

The "Oscar" joined other four ships that were lying
in Aberdeen Bay,
All ready to start for Greenland without delay,
While the hearts of each ship's crew felt light and gay,

But, when the storm burst upon them, it filled their
        hearts with dismay.

The wind had been blowing westerly during the night,
But suddenly it shifted to the North-east, and blew
        with all its might,
And thick and fast fell the blinding snow,
Which filled the poor sailors' hearts with woe.

And the "Oscar" was exposed to the full force
        of the gale,
But the crew resolved to do their best, allowing
        they should fail,
So they weighed anchor, and stood boldly out for sea,
While the great crowds that had gathered cheered
        them encouragingly.

The ill-fated "Oscar," however, sent a boat ashore
For some of her crew that were absent, while the
        angry sea did roar,
And 'twas with great difficulty the men got aboard,
And to make the ship allright they wrought with
        one accord.

Then suddenly the wind shifted, and a treacherous
        calm ensued,
And the vessel's deck with snow was thickly strewed;
And a heavy sea was running with a strong flood tide
And it soon became apparent the men wouldn't be
        able the ship to guide.

And as the "Oscar" drifted further and further
        to leeward,

The brave crew tried hard her backward drifting
        to retard,
But all their efforts proved in vain, for the storm
        broke out anew,
While the drifting snow hid her from the
        spectators' view.

And the position of the "Oscar" was critical
        in the extreme,
And as the spray washed o'er the vessel,
        O what a soul-harrowing scene!
And notwithstanding the fury of the gale and
        the blinding snow,
Great crowds watched the "Oscar" as she was
        tossed to and fro.

O heaven! it was a most heart-rending sight
To see the crew struggling against the wind and
        blinding snow with all their might,
While the mighty waves lashed her sides and
        angry did roar,
Which to their relatives were painful to see that
        were standing on shore.

All eagerly watching her attempt to ride out
        the storm,
Especially their friends and relatives, who seemed
        very forlorn,
Because the scene was awe-inspiring and made
        them stand aghast,
For every moment seemed to be the "Oscar's" last.

Oh! it was horrible to see the good ship in distress,

Battling hard against wind and tide to clear
    the Girdleness.
A conspicuous promontory on the south side of
    Aberdeen Bay,
Where many a stout ship and crew have gone
    down passing that way.

At last the vessel was driven ashore in the bay
    of Greyhope,
And the "Oscar" with the elements no longer
    could cope.
While the big waves lashed her furiously, and she
    received fearful shocks,
Until a mighty wave hurled her among large
    boulders of rocks.

And when the vessel struck, the crew stood aghast,
But they resolved to hew down the mainmast,
Which the spectators watched with eager interest,
And to make it fall on the rocks the brave sailors
    tried their best.

But, instead of falling on the rocks, it dropped into
    the angry tide,
Then a groan arose from those that were standing
    on the shore side;
And the mainmast in its fall brought down the foremast,
Then all hope of saving the crew seemed gone at last.

And a number of the crew were thrown into the
    boiling surge below,
While loud and angry the stormy wind did blow,
And the good ship was dashed to pieces

And the good ship was dashed to pieces
    from stern to stern,
Within a yard or two from their friends, who were
    powerless to save them.

Oh! it was an appalling sight to see the "Oscar"
    in distress,
While to the forecastle was seen clinging
    brave Captain Innes
And five of a crew, crying for help, which none
    could afford,
Alas! poor fellows, crying aloud to God with
    one accord!

But their cry to God for help proved all in vain,
For the ship and men sank beneath the briny main,
And out of a crew of fourty-four men, only two
    were saved,
But, landsmen, think how manfully that
    unfortunate crew behaved.

And also think of the mariners while you lie
    down to sleep,
And pray to God to protect them while on the
    briny deep,
For their hardships are many, and hard to endure,
There's only a plank between them and a watery
    grave, which makes their lives unsure.

THE CLEPINGTON CATASTROPHE

'TWAS on a Monday morning, and in the
       year of 1884,
That a fire broken out in Bailie Bradford's store,
Which contained bales of jute and large
       quantities of waste,
Which the brave firemen ran to extinguish
       in great haste.

They left their wives that morning without any dread,
Never thinking, at the burning pile, they
       would be killed dead
By the falling of the rickety and insecure walls;
When I think of it, kind Christians, my heart it appals!
Because it has caused widows and their
       families to shed briny tears,
For there hasn't been such a destructive fire
       for many years;
Whereby four brave firemen have perished
       in the fire,
And for better fathers of husbands no family
       could desire.
'Twas about five o'clock in the morning the fire
       did break out,
While one of the workmen was inspecting the
       premises round about—
Luckily before any one had begun their work
       for the day—
So he instantly gave the alarm without delay.
At that time only a few persons were gathered on
       the spot,

But in a few minutes some hundreds were got,
Who came flying in all directions, and in great dismay;
So they help'd to put out the fire without delay.

But the spreading flames, within the second flats,
          soon began to appear,
Which filled the spectators' hearts with
          sympathy and fear,
Lest anyone should lose their life in the
          merciless fire,
When they saw it bursting out and ascending
          higher and higher

Captain Ramsay, of the Dundee Fire Brigade,
          was the first to arrive,
And under his directions the men seemed all alive,
For they did their work heroically, with all their
          might and main,
In the midst of blinding smoke and the burning flame.

As soon as the catastrophe came to be known,
The words, Fire! Fire! from every mouth were blown;
And a cry of despair rang out on the morning air,
When they saw the burning pile with its red fiery glare.

While a dense cloud of smoke seemed to darken the sky,
And the red glaring flame ascended up on high,
Which made the scene appear weird-like around;
While from the spectators was heard a
          murmuring sound.

But the brave firemen did their duty manfully to the last,
And plied the water on the burning pile,

copiously and fast;
But in a moment, without warning, the front
      wall gave way,
Which filled the people's hearts with horror
      and dismay:

Because four brave firemen were killed
      instantaneously on the spot,
Which by the spectators will never be forgot;
While the Fire Fiend laughingly did hiss and roar,
As he viewed their mangled bodies, with the
      debris covered o'er.

But in the midst of dust the fire they did their
      duty well,
Aye! in the midst of a shower of bricks falling on
      them pell-mell,
Until they were compelled to let the water-hose go;
While the blood from their bruised heads
      and arms did flow.

But brave James Fyffe held on to the hose until the last,
And when found *debris*, the people stood aghast.
When they saw him lying dead, with the hose
      in his hand,
Their tears for him they couldn't check nor
      yet command.

Oh, heaven! I must confess it was no joke
To see them struggling in the midst of
      suffocating smoke,
Each man struggling hard, no doubt, to save his life,
When he thought of his dear children and his wife.

But still the merciless flame shot up higher
        and higher;
Oh, God! it is terrible and cruel to perish by fire;
Alas! it was saddening and fearful to behold,
When I think of it, kind Christians, it makes my
        blood run cold.

What makes the death of Fyffe the more   distressing,
He was going to be the groomsman at his sister's
        bridal dressing,
Who was going to be married the next day;
But, alas! the brave hero's life was taken away.

But accidents will happen by land and by sea.
Therefore, to save ourselves from accidents, we
        needn't try to flee,
For whatsoever God has ordained will come to pass;
For instance, ye may be killed by a stone or a
        piece of glass.

I hope the Lord will provide for the widows
        in their distress,
For they are to be pitied, I really must confess;
And I hope the public of Dundee will lend them a
        helping hand;
To help the widows and the fatherless is
        God's command.

THE BURNING OF THE PEOPLE'S VARIETY THEATRE, ABERDEEN

'Twas in the year of 1896, and on the 30th of September,
Which many people in Aberdeen will long remember;
The burning of the People's Variety Theatre,
    in Bridge Place,
Because the fire spread like lightning at a rapid pace.
The fire broke out on the stage, about eight o'clock,
Which gave to the audience a very fearful shock;
Then a stampede ensued, and a rush was
    made pell-mell,
And in the crush, trying to get out, many people fell.

The stage flies took fire owing to the gas
Not having room enough by them to pass;
And with his jacket Mr. Macaulay tried to
    put out the flame,
But oh! horrible to relate, it was all in vain.

Detective Innes, who was passing at the time of the fire,
Rendered help in every way the audience could desire,
By helping many of them for to get out,
Which was a heroic action, without any doubt.

Oh! it was a pitiful and fearful sight,
To see both old and young struggling with
    all their might,
For to escape from that merciless fire,
While it roared and mounted higher and higher.

Oh! it was horrible to hear the cries of that
    surging crowd,

Yelling and crying for "Help! help!" aloud;
While one old woman did fret and frown
Because her clothes were torn off when knocked down

A lady and gentleman of the Music Hall company,
    Monti & Spry,
Managed to make their escape by climbing up very high,
To an advertisement board, and smashing the
    glass of the fanlight,
And squeezed themselves through with great fight.

A little boy's leg was fractured while jumping
    from the gallery,
And by doing so he saved his life miraculously;
And every one of the artists were in a sorry plight,
Because all their properties was burnt on that night.

There were about 400 or 500 people present
    on that night,
And oh! to them it was a most appalling sight;
When the flames swept the roof at one stroke,
'Twas then that a fearful yell from the audience broke.

And in a short time the interior was one mass of flames,
And nothing but the bare walls now remains;
But thank God it did not occur on Monday night,
Or else it would have been a more pitiable sight.

Because there was an over-crowded audience on
    Monday night
The theatre was packed in every corner left and right,
Which certainly was a most pleasant sight,
And seemingly each heart was filled with delight.

The courage of Mr. T. Turner was wonderful to behold,
A private in the 92nd Highlanders, he was
 a hero bold;
Because he cast off his tunic and cap without delay,
And rescued several of the people without dismay.

Yet many were burned and disfigured in the face,
While trying hard to escape from that burning place;
Because with fear and choking smoke
Many of their hearts were almost broke.

But accidents will happen both on sea and land,
And the works of the Almighty is hard to understand;
And thank God there's only a few has fallen
 victims to the fire,
But I hope they are now in Heaven, amongst the
 Heavenly choir.

PART VI

*Now Friends of the Temperance Cause,
Follow Me.*

The Temperance Movement was one of the major popular moral crusades which blossomed during the Victorian era. The middle classes especially saw this as a necessary response to the moral degeneracy and social evils caused by alcoholism, which had become fairly widespread, particularly in the cities. They saw drunkenness and excessive expenditure on drink as one of the major causes of crime and family strife. Although this may have been true to an extent, the attribution of the working classes' poverty to their abuse of alcohol, rather than to low wages, was used to absolve the middle classes of their reponsibility. At that time many men and women worked in oppressive conditions and their home lives were little more comfortable. It is hardly surprising therefore, that some sought the short term escape from their misery which drink could provide.

In the period 1889-90 over 2000 people were convicted in Dundee of having been drunk and disorderly. Many different organisations sprung up within the Temperance movement such as the Rechabites, the Good Templars, the Band of Hope, and the Blue Ribbon Army. For some the aim was merely to moderate drinking by curbing drinking laws, for others nothing but total abstinence would suffice.

The first poem in this section **"A Tribute to Mr. Murphy**

and the Blue Ribbon Army" relates the arrival of one particular Temperance Movement which reached this country from America. Members of this cause took the pledge of total abstinence and wore a blue ribbon on their breasts, to pledge them in the face of the world to keep their promise. Although a strict teetotaller himself, McGonagall does admit in his autobiography to having been tricked into drinking alcohol. He was invited by friends to perform recitations of his work at a commemoration banquet in Dundee. The Chairman of the proceedings proposed a toast to Scotland's "Immortal and inspired poet, the great M'Gonagall". The audience were all drinking whisky, but McGonagall believed, mistakenly, that they had given him lemonade instead. He proceeded to drink his alcoholic cocktail throughout the night but eventually the "lemonade" took its toll, for he writes:

> *"I staggered to the place recently occupied by my chair, and collapsed on the floor completely 'hors de combat'. Then I awoke to consciousness with my cheek skinned, my knee bruised and found my wallet with my manuscripts gone, I firmly believed I had been poisoned at the instigation of some jealous rival; but the doctor who was called – to my utter surprise and horror – diagnosed the cause as a simple drunk and prescribed the taking of a blue pill and the pledge. I took them both, and kept the latter."*

The other poems included here – **"The Destroying Angel"**, **"The Demon Drink"** and **"A New Temperance Poem"** likewise all have strong crusading themes and reflect the moral mood of many Victorians at that time, especially in industrial cities like Dundee. Despite clearly stating his support for the Temperance movement,

McGonagall found himself in the peculiar position of performing many of his works before audiences in public houses. This apparent incongruity did not trouble him however, because he also saw his live performances in public houses as helping the cause, for *"While anyone is singing a song, or reciting, it arrests the attention of the audience from off the drink"*. On one occasion, during the Blue Ribbon Army movement in Dundee, this tactic did not go unnoticed by the landlord of the hostelry in which McGonagall was giving his recital. This particular landlord noticed that the poet was earning more from his recitations than the audience were spending on drink, and so decided to put an end to the proceedings. McGonagall writes in his autobiography: "He devised a plan to bring my entertainment to an end abruptly, and the plan was, he told the waiter to throw a wet towel at me, which, of course, the waiter did, as he was told, and I received the wet towel, full force, in the face, which staggered me, no doubt, and had the desired effect of putting an end to me giving any more entertainments in his house." The final item in this section is not one of McGonagall's poems, but rather it is one of his best known songs, and certainly one of his best pieces of writing. I have included "The Rattling Boy from Dublin" here, because it contains a line linking drink with the devil. On one occasion, a recital of this song in a village pub not far from Dundee led to one of his audience throwing peas at him. Even McGonagall managed this time to figure out what had caused such an outburst: *"The reason, I think, for the publican throwing the peas at me is because I say to the devil with your glass in my song 'The Rattling Boy from Dublin', and he no doubt considered it had a teetotal tendency, and for that reason he had felt angry and had, thrown the peas at me*." It is rather ironic that today, in his adopted home town of Dundee, one of the few outward signs of recognition of the man and his work is a public house which bears his name !

A TRIBUTE TO MR MURPHY AND
THE BLUE RIBBON ARMY

ALL hail to Mr Murphy, he is a hero brave,
That has crossed the mighty Atlantic wave,
For what purpose let me pause and think–
I answer, to warn the people not to taste strong drink.

And, I'm sure, if they take his advice, they never will rue
The day they joined the Blue Ribbon Army in
      the year 1882;
And I hope to their colours they will always
      prove true,
And shout, Hurrah! for Mr Murphy and the
      Ribbon of Blue.

What is strong drink? Let me think–I answer
      'tis a thing
From whence the majority of evils spring,
And causes many a fireside with boisterous
      talk to ring,
And leaves behind it a deadly sting.

Some people do say it is good when taken in
      moderation,
But, when taken to excess, it leads to tribulation,
Also to starvation and loss of reputation,
Likewise your eternal soul's damnation.

The drunkard, he says he can't give it up,
For I must confess temptation's in the cup;
But he wishes to God it was banished from the land,
While he holds the cup in his trembling hand.

And he exclaims in the agony of his soul—
Oh, God, I cannot myself control
From this most accurs'd cup!
Oh, help me, God, to give it up!

Strong drink to the body can do no good;
It defiles the blood, likewise the food,
And causes the drunkard with pain to groan,
Because it extracts the marrow from the bone:

And hastens him on to a premature grave,
Because to the cup he is bound a slave;
For the temptation is hard to thole,
And by it he will lose his immortal soul.

The more's the pity, I must say,
That so many men and women are by it led astray,
And decoyed from the paths of virtue and led
        on to vice
By drinking too much alcohol and acting unwise.

Good people all, of every degree,
I pray, ye all be warned by me:
I advise ye all to pause and think,
And never more to taste strong drink.

Because the drunkard shall never inherit the
        kingdom of God
And whosoever God loves he chastens with
        his rod:
Therefore be warned and think in time,
And don't drink any more whisky, rum, or wine.

But go at once– make no delay,
And join the Blue Ribbon Army without dismay,
And rally round Mr Murphy, and make a bold stand,
And help to drive the Bane of Society from our land.

I wish Mr Murphy every success,
Hoping he will make rapid progress;
And to the Blue Ribbon Army may he
     always prove true,
And adhere to his colours– the beautiful blue.

THE DESTROYING ANGEL
OR THE POET'S DREAM

I dreamt a dream the other night
That an Angel appeared to me, clothed in white.
Oh! it was a beautiful sight,
Such as filled my heart with delight.

And in her hand she held a flaming brand,
Which she waved above her head most grand;
And on me she glared with love-beaming eyes,
Then she commanded me from my bed to arise.

And in a sweet voice she said, "You must
     follow me,
And in a short time you shall see
The destruction of all the public-houses
     in the city,
Which is, my friend, the God of Heaven decree."

Then from my bed in fear I arose,
And quickly donned my clothes;
And when that was done she said, "Follow me
Direct to the High Street, fearlessly."

So with the beautiful Angel away I did go,
And when we arrived at the High Street,
    Oh! what a show.
I suppose there were about five thousand
    men there,
All vowing vengeance against the publicans,
    I do declare.

Then the Angel cried with solemn voice aloud
To that vast and Godly assembled crowd,
"Gentlemen belonging the fair City of Dundee,
Remember I have been sent here by God
    to warn ye.

"That by God's decree ye must take up arms and
    follow me
And wreck all the public-houses in this fair City,
Because God cannot countenance such dens
    of iniquity.
Therefore, friends of God, come, follow me

"Because God has said there's no use preaching
    against strong drink,
Therefore, by taking up arms against it, God
    does think,
That is the only and the effectual cure
To banish it from the land, He is quite sure.

"Besides, it has been denounced in Dundee for
    fifty years
By the friends of Temperance, while oft they
    have shed tears.
Therefore, God thinks there's no use denouncing
    it any longer,
Because the more that's said against it seemingly
    it grows stronger."

And while the Angel was thus addressing the people,
The Devil seemed to be standing on the
    Townhouse Steeple,
Foaming at the mouth with rage, and seemingly
    much annoyed,
And kicking the Steeple because the public-
    houses were going to be destroyed.

Then the Angel cried, "Satan, avaunt! begone!"
Then he vanished in the flame, to the amazement
    of everyone;
And waving aloft the flaming brand,
That she carried in her right hand.

She cried, "Now, friends of the Temperance cause,
    follow me:
For remember its God's high decree
To destroy all the public-houses in this fair City;
Therefore, friends of God, let's commence
    this war immediately."

Then from the High Street we all did retire,
As the Angel, sent by God, did desire;
And along the Perth Road we all did go,

While the Angel set fire to the public-houses
    along that row.

And when the Perth Road public-houses were
    fired, she cried, "Follow me,
And next I'll fire the Hawkhill public-houses
    instantly."
Then away we went with the Angel,
    without dread or woe,
And she fired the Hawkhill public-houses as
    onward we did go.

Then she cried, "Let's on to the Scouringburn,
    in God's name."
And away to the Scouringburn we went,
    with our hearts aflame,
As the destroying Angel did command.
And when there she fired the public-houses,
    which looked very grand.

And when the public-houses there were blazing
    like a kiln,
She cried, "Now, my friends,
    we'll march to the Bonnet Hill,
And we'll fire the dens of iniquity without dismay,
Therefore let's march on, my friends,
    without delay."

And when we arrived at the Bonnet Hill,
The Angel fired the public-houses,
    as she did well.
Then she cried, "We'll leave them now to their fate,
And march on to the Murraygate."

Then we marched on to the Murraygate,
And the Angel fired the public-houses
    there, a most deserving fate.
Then to the High Street, we marched and
    fired them there,
Which was a most beautiful blaze, I do declare.

And on the High Street, old men and women were
    gathered there,
And as the flames ascended upwards,
    in amazement they did stare
When they saw the public houses in a blaze,
But they clapped their hands with joy and to
    God gave praise.

Then the Angel cried, "Thank God, Christ's
    Kingdom's near at hand,
And there will soon be peace and plenty
    throughout the land,
And the ravages of the demon Drink no
    more will be seen."
But, alas, I started up in bed, and behold
    it was a dream!

THE DEMON DRINK

Oh, thou demon Drink, thou fell destroyer;
Thou curse of society, and its greatest annoyer.
What hast thou done to society, let me think?
I answer thou hast caused the most of ills,
    thou demon Drink.

Thou causeth the mother to neglect her child,
Also the father to act as he were wild,
So that he neglects his loving wife and family dear,
By spending his earnings foolishly on whisky,
    rum, and beer.

And after spending his earnings foolishly
    he beats his wife–
The man that promised to protect her during life–
And so the man would if there was no
    drink in society,
For seldom a man beats his wife in a state
    of sobriety.

And if he does, perhaps he finds his wife fou',
Then that causes, no doubt, a great hullaballoo;
When he finds his wife drunk he begins to frown,
And in a fury of passion he knocks her down.

And in the knock down she fractures her head,
And perhaps the poor wife is killed dead,
Whereas, if there was no strong drink to be got,
To be killed wouldn't have been the poor wife's lot.

Then the unfortunate husband is arrested and
    cast into jail,
And sadly his fate he does bewail;
And he curses the hour that ever he was born,
And paces his cell up and down very forlorn.

And when the day of his trial draws near,
No doubt for the murdering of his wife he
    drops a tear,

And he exclaims, "Oh, thou demon Drink,
 through thee I must die,"
And on the scaffold he warns the people
 from drink to fly,

Because whenever a father or a mother
 takes to drink,
Step by step on in crime they do sink,
Until their children loses all affection for them,
And in justice we cannot their children condemn.

The man that gets drunk is little else than a fool,
And is in the habit, no doubt, of advocating for
 Home Rule;
But the best Home Rule for him,
 as far as I can understand,
Is the abolition of strong drink from the land.

And the men that get drunk in general wants
 Home Rule;
But such men, I rather think, should keep
 their heads cool,
And try and learn more sense, I most earnestly do pray,
And help to get strong drink abolished
 without delay.

If drink was abolished how many peaceful
 homes would there be,
Just, for instance, in the beautiful town of Dundee;
Then this world would be a haven, whereas it's a hell,
And the people would have more peace
 in it to dwell.

Alas! strong drink makes men and women fanatics,
And helps to fill our prisons and lunatics;
And if there was no strong drink such
      cases wouldn't be,
Which would be a very glad sight for all
      Christians to see.

I admit, a man may be a very good man,
But in my opinion he cannot be a true Christian
As long as he partakes of strong drink,
The more that he may differently think.

But, no matter what he thinks, I say nay,
For by taking it he helps to lead his brother astray,
Whereas, if he didn't drink, he would help to
      reform society,
And we would soon do away with all inebriety.

Then, for the sake of society and the Church of God,
Let each one try to abolish it at home and abroad;
Then poverty and crime would decrease and
      be at a stand,
And Christ's Kingdom would soon be established
      throughout the land.

Therefore, brothers and sisters, pause and think,
And try to abolish the foul fiend, Drink.
Let such doctrine be taught in church and school,
That the abolition of strong drink is the only
      Home Rule.

A NEW TEMPERANCE POEM,

IN MEMORY OF MY DEPARTED PARENTS, WHO WERE SOBER LIVING & GOD FEARING PEOPLE.

My parents were sober living, and often did pray,
For their family to abstain from intoxicating
    drink away;
Because they knew it would lead them astray,
Which no God fearing man will dare gainsay.

Some people do say that God made strong drink,
But he is not so cruel I think;
To lay a stumbling block in his children's way,
And then punish them for going astray.

No! God has more love for his children,
    than mere man
To make strong drink their souls to damn;
His love is more boundless than mere man's by far,
And to say not it would be an unequal par.

A man that truly loves his family wont allow
    them to drink,
Because he knows seldom about God they
    will think,
Besides he knows it will destroy their intellect,
And cause them to hold their parents in disrespect.

Strong drink makes the people commit all
    sorts of evil,
And must have been made by the Devil

For to make them quarrel, murder, steal, and fight,
And prevent them from doing what is right.

The Devil delights in leading the people astray,
So that he may fill his kingdom with them
     without delay;
It is the greatest pleasure he can really find,
To be the enemy of all mankind.

The Devil delights in breeding family strife,
Especially betwixt man and wife;
And if the husband comes home drunk at night,
He laughs and crys, ha! ha! what a beautiful sight.

And if the husband asks his supper when he
     comes in,
The poor wife must instantly find it for him;
And if she cannot find it, he will curse and frown,
And very likely knock his loving wife down.

Then the children will scream aloud,
And the Devil no doubt will feel very proud,
If he can get the children to leave their own
     fireside,
And to tell their drunken father,
     they won't with him reside.

Strong drink will cause the gambler to rob
     and kill his brother,
Aye! also his father and his mother,
All for the sake of getting money to gamble,
Likewise to drink, cheat, and wrangle.

And when the burglar wants to do his work
  very handy,
He plies himself with a glass of Whisky, Rum,
  or Brandy,
To give himself courage to rob and kill,
And innocent people's blood to spill.

Whereas if he couldn't get Whisky, Rum,
  or Brandy,
He wouldn't do his work so handy;
Therefore, in that respect let strong drink be
  abolished in time,
And that will cause a great decrease in crime.

Therefore, for this sufficient reason remove it
  from society,
For seldom burglary is committed in a state
  of sobriety;
And I earnestly entreat ye all to join with
  heart and hand,
And to help to chase away the Demon drink
  from bonnie Scotland.

I beseech ye all to kneel down and pray,
And implore God to take it away;
Then this world would be a heaven,
  whereas it is a hell,
And the people would have more peace in it
  to dwell.

THE RATTLING BOY FROM DUBLIN

I'M a rattling boy from Dublin town,
I courted a girl called Biddy Brown,
Her eyes they were as black as sloes,
She had black hair and an aquiline nose.

Chorus-
Whack fal de da, fal de darelido,
Whack fak de da, fal de darelay,
Whack fal de da, fal de darelido,
Whack fal de da, fal de darelay.

One night I met with another lad,
Says, I, Biddy, I've caught you, by dad;
I never thought you were half so bad
As to be going about with another lad.
  Chorus.

Says I, Biddy, this will never do,
For to-night you've prov'd to me untrue,
So do not make a hullaballoo,
For I will bid farewell to you.
  Chorus.

Says Barney Magee, She is my lass,
And the man that says no, he is an ass,
So come away, and I'll give you a glass,
Och, sure you can get another lass.
  Chorus.

Says I, to the devil with your glass,
You have taken from me my darling lass,

And if you look angry, or offer to frown,
With my darling shillelah I'll knock you down.
  Chorus.

Says Barney Magee unto me,
By the hokey I love Biddy Brown,
And before I'll give her up to thee,
One or both of us will go down.
  Chorus.

So, with my darling shillelah, I gave him a whack,
Which left him lying on his back,
Saying, botheration to you and Biddy Brown,—
For I'm the rattling boy from Dublin town.
  Chorus.

So a policeman chanced to come up at the time,
And he asked of me the cause of the shine,
Says I, he threatened to knock me down
When I challenged him for walking with my
  Biddy Brown.
  Chorus.

So the policeman took Barney Magee to jail,
Which made him shout and bewail
That ever he met with Biddy Brown,
The greatest deceiver in Dublin town.
  Chorus.

So I bade farewell to Biddy Brown,
The greatest jilter in Dublin town,
Because she proved untrue to me,
And was going about with Barney Magee.

PART VII

*Ye Sons of Great Britain, Come Join with Me /
Twas in the Year....*

Battles provide dramatic subjects for any poet, and one with a dramatic bent such as McGonagall must have delighted in reciting his own poems, so full of patriotic verve, with due gusto. The poems may still not be great, but no one can fail but be impressed by the underlying force and passion which runs through them. At least in his poetry, McGonagall could occasionally be on the winning side.

In fact, McGonagall claimed to have a military background himself. He said that he had served in the Perthshire Militia as a young man, although, true to his somewhat sketchy history, no actual records of his service have ever been found. No doubt he would have made a doughty soldier, not only because of his unswerving patriotism, but because of his willingness to fight for a cause even in the face of overwhelming odds. McGonagall's personal life was one such long battle.

The "battle" poems which he wrote fall broadly into two categories historical and journalistic. From the first of these categories I include here McGonagall's accounts of the Battles of Bannockburn and Culloden. **"The Battle of Bannockburn"** is perhaps McGonagall's most famous historical poem, which he delighted in performing upon the stage, dressed in his "Celtic garb", sometimes with disastrous consequences. We learn from a local newspaper dated April 1881 of how his "Battle of Bannockburn" was received at the Masonic Hall in Montrose:

"The climax was reached however when the McGonagall, sword in hand, was singing a terrific battle piece. The bump of combativeness became so simultaneously roused in the heads of all the 'chosen spirits' that they commenced attacking the lecturer and each other from a bag of flour......"

According to John Willocks' "autobiographical" sketches of McGonagall, he met with similar results in his home town of Dundee. Here he was offered a weeks trial engagement by Baron Ziegler who ran a variety entertainment at an old circus at the back of the Queen's Hotel. He writes:

"It did, indeed, prove a trial for both of us. The first night I appeared there certainly was a little undue excitement amongst the audience; and some throwing of objectionable and dangerous missiles; but on the whole I was allowed to proceed in comparative peace with my famous 'Bannockburn', which was applauded to the echo. Next night however – shall I ever forget it ? Never ! I shall carry its memory as well as its marks to the grave. Until that night I never for a moment imagined that there were so many veritable fiends in all Europe, let alone Dundee......As soon as I emerged from under it, and had just reached the platform arrayed in my Celtic garb, with sword and buckler complete, strutting as proud as a peacock, a whole big jute bag full of soot was emptied right over me."

Things went from "bad to verse", with the audience throwing boots, beef tins, rotten eggs and even bricks at the poet, before a full scale riot broke out. Sadly for McGonagall, "Bannockburn" did not prove as successful as it had been for Robert the Bruce in 1314, athough he did seem to take on board the "try and try again" philosophy!

I also include here McGonagall's historical poem about **"The Battle of Culloden"**. It fits in perfectly with the Victorian preoccupation, led by the Queen herself, with the romanticised and sentimental memory of Jacobitism, clans, tartans and of all things "Scottish". No doubt the ill-fated Bonnie Prince Charlie was another tragic character with whom the poet could identify.

McGonagall's other "Battle" poems related largely to the current events of his day and took the form of journalistic accounts of the exploits of "brave British soldiers". They reflect the strong Victorian preoccupation with battles which were fought in the name of the Empire, the purpose of which was to bring so-called civilisation to the "natives". Between 1882 and 1889, when McGonagall was writing, British forces were involved in the Egyptian and Sudanese Campaign. At the beginning of the nineteenth century, most of Africa was still unknown to the Europeans. However between 1877 and 1914, almost the entire continent of Africa was hurriedly colonised by the major European powers – a process which has been called "The Scramble for Africa". Apart from various powerful nations wanting to extend their spheres of influence, rapid industrialisation in Europe had created a demand for new markets and raw materials – Africa provided both.

Britain in which McGonagall lived was certainly no exception – the Victorian era saw the country's Colonial Empire reach its maximum, both in terms of size and power. At that time Egypt was still nominally a part of the Turkish Empire. Britain however had a vested interest in its stability as it had a half share in the Suez Canal, which was vital to the trade route to India and the Far East. Eventually after a rebellion led by Achmet Arabi Pasha, the British stepped in to restore order. Mr. Gladstone, the Prime Minister, reluctantly agreed to military action which culminated in **"The Battle of Tel el Kebir"**. This battle which McGonagall dramatically unfolds for us took place on the 13th September 1882. He must have gleaned all the details from newspaper accounts at the time, for he certainly never set foot in Africa.

The British troops were supposed to be withdrawn after this victory, however a series of troubles broke out in the Sudan, which was considered a province of Egypt at that time. Although the British Government did not want to be involved in an expensive war in the Sudan, the threat to the stability of Egypt forced them to embark on a reconquest of the Sudan. McGonagall's poem **"The Battle of El Teb"** relates the incidents which took place in one of the battles which occurred during the Sudan Campaign between the forces of Major General Sir Gerald Graham and Osman Digna, the Mahdist Governor of Eastern Sudan. The battle took place on the 29th February 1884, and McGonagall sent copies of his poem to Lord Wolseley on the 7th April, for which he received an acknowledgement courtesy of the War Office. He was very proud of this acceptance, and used to print "Patronised by Her Majesty, and Lord Wolseley of Cairo, H.R.H the Duke of Cambridge, The Rt. Hon. W.E. Gladstone and General Graham" at the top of his broadsheets.

The final poem in this section recounts **"The Battle of Omdurman"** which took place on the 2nd September 1898, and saw the eventual reconquest of the Sudan by the British. In this battle the British were led by General Sir Herbert Kitchener against the Khalifa Abdullah's army. One of the best remembered episodes in the Battle which McGonagall relates, was the charge of the 21st Lancers, in which Lieutenant Winston Churchill (later M.P. for Dundee and Prime Minister) took part.

Although McGonagall wrote about many different battles, in many different lands throughout the Empire, I think that the patronage which he received from Lord Wolseley and General Graham for these poems about the Egyptian-Sudan Campaign gave him especial pleasure.

And so to battle !

THE BATTLE OF BANNOCKBURN

Sir Robert the Bruce at Bannockburn
Beat the English in every wheel and turn,
And made them fly in great dismay
From off the field without delay.

The English were a hundred thousand strong,
And King Edward passed through the Lowlands
    all along,
Determined to conquer Scotland, it was his desire,
And then to restore it to his own empire.

King Edward brought numerous waggons in his train,
Expecting that most of the Scottish army would
    be slain,
Hoping to make the rest prisoners, and carry them away
In waggon-loads to London without delay.

The Scottish army did not amount to more than
    thirty thousand strong;
But Bruce had confidence he'd conquer his
    foes ere long;
So, to protect his little army, he thought it was right
To have deep-dug pits made in the night;

And caused them to be overlaid with turf and
    brushwood
Expecting the plan would prove effectual
    where his little army stood,
Waiting patiently for the break of day,
All willing to join in the deadly fray.

Bruce stationed himself at the head of the reserve,
Determined to conquer, but never to swerve,
And by his side were brave Kirkpatrick and
      true De Longueville,
Both trusty warriors, firm and bold,
      who would never him beguile.

By daybreak the whole of the English army
      came in view,
Consisting of archers and horsemen, bold and true;
The main body was led on by King Edward himself,
An avaricious man, and fond of pelf.

The Abbot of Inchaffray celebrated mass,
And all along the Scottish lines barefoot he did pass,
With the crucifix in his hand, a most beautiful
      sight to see,
Exhorting them to trust in God,
      and He would set them free.

Then the Scottish army knelt down on the field,
And King Edward he thought they were going to yield,
And he felt o'erjoyed, and cried to Earl Percy,
"See! See! the Scots are crying for mercy."

But Percy said, "Your Majesty need not make
      such a fuss,
They are crying for mercy from God, not from us;
For, depend upon it, they will fight to a man,
      and find their graves
Rather than yield to become your slaves."

Then King Edward ordered his horsemen to charge,
Thirty thousand in number, it was very large;
They thought to o'erwhelm them ere they
     could rise from their knees,
But they met a different destiny,
     which did them displease;
For the horsemen fell into the spik'd pits in the way,
And, with broken ranks and confusion,
     they all fled away.

But few of them escap'd death from the spik'd pits,
For the Scots with their swords hack'd them to bits;
De Valance was overthrown and carried off the field,
Then King Edward he thought it was time to yield.

And he uttered a fearful cry
To his gay archers near by,
Ho! archers! draw your arrows to the head,
And make sure to kill them dead;
Forward, without dread, and make them fly,
Saint George for England, be our cry!

Then the arrows from their bows swiftly did go,
And fell amongst them as thick as the flakes of snow;
Then Bruce he drew his trusty blade,
And in heroic language said,
Forward! my heroes, bold and true!
And break the archers' ranks through and through!
And charge them boldly with your swords in hand,
And chase these vultures from off our land,
And make King Edward mourn
The day he came to Bannockburn.

So proud Edward on his milk-white steed,
One of England's finest breed,
Coming here in grand array,
With horsemen bold and archers gay,
Thinking he will us dismay,
And sweep everything before him in his way;
But I swear by yon blessed sun
I'll make him and his army run
From off the field of Bannockburn.

By St. Andrew and our God most high,
We'll conquer these epicures or die!
And make them fly like chaff before the wind
Until they can no refuge find;
And beat them off the field without delay,
Like lions bold and heroes gay.
Upon them!– charge!– follow me,
For Scotland's rights and liberty!

Then the Scots charged them with sword inhand,
And made them fly from off their land;
And King Edward was amazed at the sight,
And he got wounded in the fight;
And he cried, Oh, heaven! England's lost,
   and I'm undone,
Alas! alas! where shall I run?
Then he turned his horse, and rode on afar,
And never halted till he reached Dunbar.

Then Bruce he shouted, Victory!
We have gained our rights and liberty;
And thanks be to God above
That we have conquered King Edward this day,

A usurper that does not us love.
Then the Scots did shout and sing,
Long live Sir Robert Bruce our King!
That made King Edward mourn
The day he came to Bannockburn!

THE BATTLE OF CULLODEN:
A HISTORICAL POEM

'TWAS in the year of 1746, and in April the 14th day,
That Prince Charles and his army marched on
    without delay,
And on the 14th of April they encamped on
    Culloden Moor,
But the army felt hungry, and no food could
    they procure.

And the calls of hunger could not brook delay,
So they resolved to have food, come what may;
They, poor men, were hungry and in sore distress,
And many of them, as well as officers,
    slipped off to Inverness.

The Prince gave orders to bring provisions to
    the field,
Because he knew without food his men would
    soon yield
To the pangs of hunger, besides make them feel
    discontent,
So some of them began to search the neigh-
    bourhood for refreshment.

And others, from exhaustion, lay down on the
    ground,
And soon in the arms of Morpheus they were
    sleeping sound;
While the Prince and some of his officers began
    to search for food,
And got some bread and whisky,
    which they thought very good.

The Highland army was drawn up in three lines
    in grand array,
All eager for the fray in April the 16th day,
Consisting of the Athole Brigade,
    who made a grand display
On the field of Culloden on that ever-
    memorable day.

Likewise the Camerons, Stewarts, and Mac-
    intoshes, Maclachlans and Macleans,
And John Roy Stewart's regiment,
    united into one, these are their names;
Besides the Macleods, Chisholms, Macdonalds
    of Clanranald and Glengarry,
Also the noble chieftain Keppoch,
    all eager the English to harry.

The second line of the Highland army formed
    in column on the right,
Consisting of the Gordons, under Lord Lewis
    Gordon, ready for the fight;
Besides the French Royal Scots, the Irish
    Piquets or Brigade,
Also Lord Kilmarnock's Foot Guards,

and a grand show they made.

Lord John Drummond's regiment and
     Glenbucket's were flanked on the right
By Fitz-James's Dragoons and Lord Elcho's
     Horse Guards, a magnificent sight;
And on the left by the Perth squadron under
     Lord Strathallan,
A fine body of men, and resolved to fight to a man.

And there was Pitsligo, and the Prince's body
     guards under Lord Balmerino,
And the third line was commanded by General
     Stapleton, a noble hero;
Besides, Lord Ogilvie was in command of the
     third line or reserve,
Consisting of the Duke of Perth's regiment and
     Lord Ogilvy's– men of firm nerve.

The Prince took his station on a very
     small eminence,
Surrounded by a troop of Fitz-James's horse
     for his defence,
Where he had a complete view of the whole
     field of battle,
Where he could see the front line and hear the
     cannons rattle.

Both armies were about the distance of a mile
     from each other,
All ready to commence the fight,
     brother against brother,
Each expecting that the other would advance

To break a sword in combat, or shiver a lance.

To encourage his men the Duke of Cumberland
    rode along the line,
Addressing himself hurriedly to every
    regiment, which was really sublime;
Telling his men to use their bayonets,
    and allow the Highlanders to mingle with them,
And look terror to the rebel foe,
    and have courage, my men.

Then Colonel Belford of the Duke's army
    opened fire from the front line,
After the Highlanders had been firing for a
    short time;
The Duke ordered Colonel Belford to continue
    the cannonade,
To induce the Highlanders to advance,
    because they seemed afraid.

And with a cannon-ball the Prince's horse was
    shot above the knee,
So that Charles had to change him for another
    immediately;
And one of his servants who led the horse was
    killed on the spot,
Which by Prince Charles Stuart was never forgot.

'Tis said in history, before the battle began
The Macdonalds claimed the right as their due
    of leading the van,
And because they wouldn't be allowed,
    with anger their hearts did burn,

Because Bruce conferred that honour upon the
    Macdonalds at the Battle of Bannockburn.

And galled beyond endurance by the fire of the
    English that day,
Which caused the Highlanders to cry aloud to
    be led forward without delay,
Until at last the brave Clan Macintosh rushed
    forward without dismay,
While with grape-shot from a side battery
    hundreds were swept away.

Then, the Athole Highlanders and the Camerons
    rushed in sword in hand,
And broke through Barrel's and Monro's
    regiments, a sight most grand;
After breaking through these two regiments
    they gave up the contest,
Until at last they had to retreat after doing their best.

Then, stung to the quick, the brave Keppoch,
    who was abandoned by his clan,
Boldly advanced with his drawn sword in hand,
    the brave man.
But, alas! he was wounded by a musket-shot,
    which he manfully bore,
And in the fight he received another shot,
    and fell to rise no more.

Nothing could be more disastrous to the Prince that day,
Owing to the Macdonalds refusing to join in
    the deadly fray;
Because if they had all shown their wonted

courage that day,
The proud Duke of Cumberland's army would
        have been forced to run away.

And, owing to the misconduct of the Macdonalds,
        the Highlanders had to yield,
And General O'Sullivan laid hold of Charles's
        horse, and led him off the field,
As the whole army was now in full retreat,
And with the deepest concern the Prince
        lamented his sore defeat.

Prince Charles Stuart, of frame and renown,
You might have worn Scotland's crown,
If the Macdonalds and Glengarry at Culloden
        had proved true;
But, being too ambitious for honour, that they didn't do,
Which, I am sorry to say, proved most disastrous
        to you,
Looking to the trials and struggles you passed through.

THE BATTLE OF TEL-EL-KEBIR

YE sons of Great Britain, come join with me,
And sing in praise of Sir Garnet Wolseley;
Sound drums and trumpets cheerfully,
For he has acted most heroically.

Therefore loudly his praises sing
Until the hills their echoes back doth ring;
For he is a noble hero bold,
And an honour to his Queen and country, be it told.

He has gained for himself fame and renown,
Which to posterity will be handed down;
Because he has defeated Arabi by land and by sea,
And from the battle of Tel-el-Kebir he made him to flee.

With an army about fourteen thousand strong,
Through Egypt he did fearlessly march along,
With the gallant and brave Highland brigade,
To whom honour is due, be it said.

Arabi's army was about seventy thousand in all,
And, virtually speaking, it wasn't very small;
But if they had been as numerous again,
The Irish and Highland brigades would have
        beaten them, it is plain.

'Twas on the 13th day of September, in the year of 1882,
Which Arabi and his rebel horde long will rue;
Because Sir Garnet Wolseley and his brave little band
Fought and conquered them on Kebir land.

He marched upon the enemy with his gallant band
O'er the wild and lonely desert sand,
And attacked them before daylight,
And in twenty minutes he put them to flight.

The first shock of the attack was borne by the
        Second Brigade,
Who behaved most manfully, it is said,
Under the command of brave General Grahame,
And have gained a lasting honour to their name.

But Major Hart and the 18th Royal Irish,conjoint,
Carried the trenches at the bayonet point;
Then the Marines chased them about four miles away,
At the charge of the bayonet, without dismay!

General Sir Archibald Alison led on the
     Highland Brigade,
Who never were the least afraid.
And such has been the case in this Egyptian war,
For at the charge of the bayonet they ran from
     them afar!

With their bagpipes playing, and one ringing cheer,
And the 42nd soon did the trenches clear;
Then hand to hand they did engage,
And fought like tigers in a cage.

Oh! it must have been a glorious sight
To see Sir Garnet Wolseley in the thickest of the fight!
In the midst of shot and shell, and the cannon's roar,
Whilst the dead and the dying lay weltering in
     their gore.

Then the Egyptians were forced to yield,
And the British were left masters of the field;
Then Arabi he did fret and frown
To see his army thus cut down.

Then Arabi the rebel took a flight,
And spurred his Arab steed with all his might:
With his heart full of despair and woe,
And never halted till he reached Cairo.

Now since the Egyptian war is at an end,
Let us thank God! Who did send
Sir Garnet Wolseley to crush and kill
Arabi and his rebel army at Kebir hill.

THE BATTLE OF EL-TEB

YE sons of Great Britain, I think no shame
To write in praise of brave General Graham!
Whose name will be handed down to posterity
    without any stigma,
Because, at the battle of El-Teb,
    he defeated Osman Digna.

With an army about five thousand strong,
To El-Teb, in the year 1884, he marched along,
    and bivouacked there for the night;
While around their fires they only thought of
    the coming fight.

They kept up their fires all the long night,
Which made the encampment appear weird-
    like to the sight;
While men were completely soaked with the rain,
But the brave heroes disdained to complain.

The brave heroes were glad when daylight did appear,
And when the reveille was sounded, they gave
    a hearty cheer
And their fires were piled up higher again,
Then they tried to dry their clothes that were
    soaked with the rain.

Then breakfast was taken about eight o'clock,
And when over, each man stood in the ranks as
    firm as a rock,
And every man seemed to be on his guard–
All silent and ready to move forward.

The first movement was a short one from
    where they lay–
Then they began to advance towards El-Teb
    without dismay,
And showed that all was in order for the fray,
While every man's heart seemed to feel light and gay.

The enemy's position could be seen in the
    distance far away
But the brave heroes marched on without delay–
Whilst the enemy's banners floated in the air,
And dark swarms of men were scattered near by there.

Their force was a large one– its front extended
    over a mile,
And all along the line their guns were all in file;
But as the British advanced, they disappeared,
While our brave kilty lads loudly cheered.

Thus slowly and cautiously brave General
    Graham proceeded
And to save his men from slaughter,
    great caution was needed,
Because Osman Digna's force was about ten
    thousand strong;
But he said, Come on, my brave lads,
    we'll conquer them ere long!

It was about ten o'clock when they came near the
    enemy's lines,
And on the morning air could be heard the cheerful
    chimes
Coming from the pipes of the gallant Black Watch,
Which every ear in the British force was eager to
    catch.

Then they passed by the enemy about mid-day,
While every Arab seemed to have his gun ready
    for the fray
When a bullet strikes down General Baker by the
    way,
But he is soon in the saddle again without delay.

And ready for any service that he could perform;
Whilst the bullets fell around them in a perfect
    storm
That they had to lie down but not through fear,
Because the enemy was about 800 yards on their
    left rear.

Then General Graham addressed his men,
And said, If they won't attack us,
    we must attack them,
So start to your feet, my lads, and never fear,
And strike up your bagpipes, and give a loud cheer.

So they leapt to their feet, and gave a loud cheer,
While the Arabs swept down upon them
    without the least fear,
And put aside their rifles, and grasped their spears;

Whilst the British bullets in front of them the
      earth uptears.

Then the British charged them with their cold steel,
Which made the Arabs backward for to reel;
But they dashed forward again on their ranks
      without dismay,
But before the terrible fire of their musketry
      they were swept away.

Oh, God of Heaven! it was a terrible sight
To see, and hear the Arabs shouting with all
      their might
A fearful oath when they got an inch of cold steel,
Which forced them backwards again,
      and made them reel.

By two o'clock they were fairly beat,
And Osman Digna, the false prophet,
      was forced to retreat
After three hours of an incessant fight;
But Heaven, 'tis said, defends the right.

And I think he ought to be ashamed of himself;
For I consider he has acted the part of a silly elf,
By thinking to conquer the armies of the Lord
With his foolish and benighted rebel horde.

THE BATTLE OF OMDURMAN

YE Sons of Great Britain! come join with me
And sing in praise of the gallant British Armie,
That behaved right manfully in the Soudan,
At the great battle of Omdurman.

'Twas in the year of 1898, and on the 2nd of
    September,
Which the Khalifa and his surviving followers
    will long remember,
Because Sir Herbert Kitchener has annihilated
    them outright,
By the British troops and Soudanese in the
    Omdurman fight.

The Sirdar and his Army left the camp in grand
    array,
And marched on to Omdurman without delay,
Just as the brigades had reached the crest
    adjoining the Nile,
And became engaged with the enemy in military style.

The Dervishes had re-formed under cover of a
    rocky eminence,
Which to them, no doubt, was a strong defence,
And they were massed together in battle array
Around the black standard of the Khalifa,
    which made a grand display.

But General Maxwell's Soudanese brigade
    seized the eminence in a short time,
And General Macdonald's brigade then joined

the firing line;
And in ten minutes, long before the attack
    could be driven home,
The flower of the Khalifa's army was almost
    overthrown.

Still manfully the dusky warriors strove to
    make headway,
But the Soudanese troops and British swept
    them back without dismay,
And their main body were mown down by
    their deadly fire—
But still the heroic Dervishes refused to retire.

And defiantly they planted their standards
    and died by them,
To their honour be it said, just like brave men;
But at last they retired, with their hearts full
    of woe,
Leaving the field white with corpses,
    like a meadow dotted with snow.

The chief heroes in the fight were the 21st Lancers;
They made a brilliant charge on the enemy
    with ringing cheers,
And through the dusky warriors bodies their
    lances they did thrust,
Whereby many of them were made to lick the dust.

Then at a quarter past eleven the Sirdar sounded
    the advance,
And the remnant of the Dervishes fled,
    which was their only chance,

While the cavalry cut off their retreat while
    they ran;
Then the Sirdar, with the black standard of the
    Khalifa, headed for Omdurman.

And when the Khalifa saw his noble army cut
    down,
With rage and grief he did fret and frown;
Then he spurred his noble steed, and swiftly it ran,
While inwardly to himself he cried,
    "Catch me if you can!"

And Mahdism now has received a crushing blow,
For the Khalifa and his followers have met
    with a complete overthrow;
And General Gordon has been avenged,
    the good Christian,
By the defeat of the Khalifa at the battle of
    Omdurman.

Now since the Khalifa has been defeated and
    his rule is at an end,
Let us thank God that fortunately did send
The brave Sir Herbert Kitchener to conquer
    that bad man,
The inhuman Khalifa, and his followers at
    the battle of Omdurman.

Success to Sir Herbert Kitchener!
    he is a great commander,
And as skilful in military tactics as the great
    Alexander,

Because he devised a very wise plan,
And by it has captured the town of Omdurman.

I wish success to the British and Soudanese Army,
May God protect them by land and by sea,
May he enable them always to conquer the foe,
And to establish what's right wherever they go.

SELECT BIBLIOGRAPHY

1. McGonagall, William. **Collected Poems.**
Omnibus Edition, Birlinn Ltd. 1992*

2. Willocks, John. **Autobiography of William McGonagall.** Dundee, 1905

3. Henderson, Hamish. "McGonagall the What".
In **Alias MacAlias.** Polygon, 1992

4. Phillips, David. **McGonagall and Tommy Atkins.** D. Winter & Son Ltd.,
Dundee 1973.

5. **The Concise Dictionary of National Biography.** Oxford University Press, Oxford. 1992

6. Martin, G.M. **Dundee Worthies.**
D. Winter & Son, Dundee 1934.

7. Marshall, D. **The Life and Times of Victoria.** Weidenfield & Nicolson, London. 1992

* Containing: Poetic Gems of Willian McGonagall,
More Poetic Gems of Willian McGonagall,
and Last Poetic Gems of William McGonagall, all published
originally by D. Winter & Son, Ltd., Dundee.

"This contribution to the literature of the 19th century was evidently the work of a modest genius who was unwarrantably hiding his light under a bushel."

Weekly News

"I earnestly hope the inhabitants of the beautiful city of Dundee,
Will appreciate this little volume got by me,
And when they read its pages, I hope it will fill their hearts with delight
While seated around the fireside on a cold winter's night;
And some of them, no doubt, will let a silent tear fall
In dear remembrance of
William McGonagall"

This selected Edition brings together the best, or worst, of McGonagall's poems taken from the three famous collections - Poetic Gems, More Poetic Gems and Last Poetic Gems.

As well as including his most famous works this volume includes autobiographical sketches and historical notes to help the reader find the true McGonagall. This new pocket volume is truly -
THE ESSENTIAL McGONAGALL
for devotee and novice alike.